AUSTIN ROCK

Jordan DeLong on "Lucky Strikes". Photo by Sean O'Grady

Austin Rock

Rock Hound Printing
erockguide@hotmail.com
www.erockonline.com

FIRST EDITION

Third Printing (2008)

Cataloging-in-Publication Data

O'Grady, Sean
Austin Rock

ISBN 978-0-9772834-0-8 Pbk

Printed in the United States of America
At Morgan Printing in Austin, Texas
Published by Rock Hound in Austin, Texas

AustinRock
ErockOnline.com

WARNING: CLIMBING IS A SPORT WHERE YOU MAY BE SERIOUSLY INJURED OR DIE. READ THIS BEFORE VENTURING INTO THIS BOOK!

This guidebook is a compilation of information acquired from many different sources and individuals. While every attempt has been made to ensure the accuracy of the information contained in these pages, there is no guarantee that this guide is accurate or up to date. The route descriptions, ratings, topos, approach information, and first ascent information may be misleading or incorrect. If you are unsure of your ability to climb a particular route, do not continue. If you do not know which way the route goes, and are unsure of your safety, do not continue. Do not rely on this guide to ensure your safety. You could get seriously injured and/or die. If you do not want to assume these risks, go play golf!

THE AUTHOR, PUBLISHER, AND PRINTER EXPRESSLY DISCLAIM ALL REPRESENTATIONS AND WARRANTIES REGARDING THIS GUIDE, THE ACCURACY OF THE INFORMATION HEREIN, AND THE RESULTS OF YOUR USE, INCLUDING WITHOUT LIMITATION, IMPLIED WARRANTIES OF MERCHANTABILITY AND FITNESS FOR A PARTICULAR PURPOSE. THE USER ASSUMES ALL RISK ASSOCIATED WITH THE USE OF THIS GUIDE. YOU ARE RESPONSIBLE FOR YOUR OWN CLIMBING SAFETY.

TABLE OF CONTENTS

PREFACE

Austin is, in my opinion, the greatest city in Texas a climber can live. There is plenty to do, both indoors and outdoors. We have a real greenbelt, and several state parks within a stones through of each other. For a climber, Austin is as close to Utopia as one can come.

I moved to Austin in 2000 for the sole purpose of climbing. I remember being so excited to get down to Seismic (Maggy's) Wall the first day I got here that I didn't even bother unpacking first. I figured it had to be a dream to live and work so close to such great climbing, that if I didn't hurry, the walls would disappear before I got there. That excitement hasn't faded. Every chance I get to go climbing, I'm super excited and stoked to get on the rock. The climbing community in Austin is also something of mention. Everyone is nice, willing to give beta, willing to clean your route if you get in over your head and willing to share a beer afterwards.

Austin is truly the greatest city in Texas, and you now have the key to its climbing. Have a great time, and be safe!

ACKNOWLEDGEMENTS

When writing this guide to Austin climbing, I came to consider myself more of a composer than an author. Like the guy standing in front of his orchestra, waving his arms frantically while those playing the instruments are the ones who are actually making the music, I too am no more than a composer and conductor, while the orchestra created this wonderful book. This guide has been a group effort, and absolutely could not have been even half as good without the help of my close friends; those who know more beta on more routes than I will ever know. Thank you very much.

| Luke Bowman | Jordan Delong | Rick Watson | Kirk Holladay |
| Tommy Blackwell | Pete Bishop | Jeff Olson | Scott Isgitt |

Also, most of the photos in this guide have been taken by photographers who have donated their work to this guide. Thank you very much for you contribution. (All un-labeled photos were taken by Sean O'Grady)

| Mario Cantu | Tim Stich | John Beveridge | Tommy Blackwell |
| Tom Suhler | | Merrick Ales (merrickales.com) | |

Jordan DeLong getting started on "Body Wax"

OVERVIEW MAP

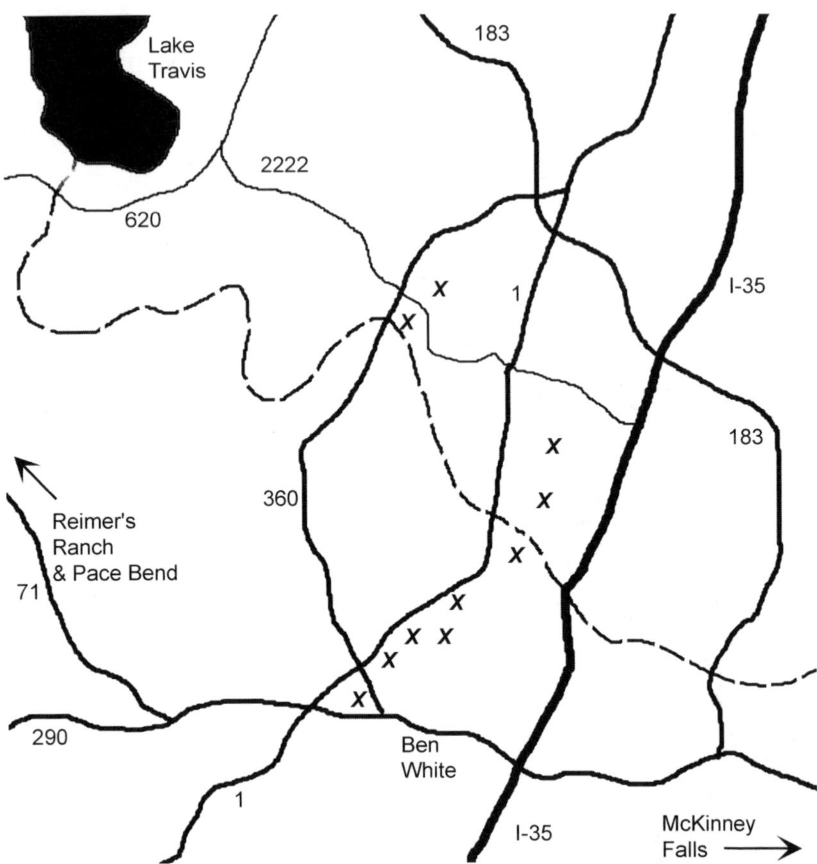

INTRODUCTION

The climbing in and around Austin ranks on par with some of the world class climbing destinations, albeit a bit shorter. Very few places will allow you to get some hard climbing in over your lunch break like Austin. There are hundreds of bolted sport routes, and just as many boulder problems scattered throughout the city, that one could literally spend a lifetime here and never get to all of the problems and routes

AustinRock
ErockOnline.com

that are available. If you are here for only a couple days, you are in for a treat. This book will hopefully guide you effortlessly to the greatest of the great with little effort, in order that you may make the most of your time.

The climbing season in Austin is basically all year long. The hot summers and cold winters don't usually deter most folks, and there are many places to retreat so that you can be guarded from the elements, even on the most inclement of days. Many of the walls around Austin resemble an outdoor gym, grid bolted so that route finding can be difficult. Deciding whether to go left or right to the bolt that's two feet away, or go straight up to the bolt that is three feet away can sometimes be a tough decision. If you get lost on a route, a local can probably show you the way.

Be aware of these hazards while climbing on Austin limestone:

Fixed Protection: Most of the bolts and anchors are well maintained by the CTM (Central Texas Mountaineers) but there is always a chance that the bolt you clip is a rusty spinner. Don't blindly accept the bolts you clip as bomber. If you question the pro, back off the route.

Route Descriptions: While every effort has been made to make the descriptions in this book accurate, they may still contain some incorrect information. If you are unsure of where to go or what to do, get qualified help. Don't just dash forward based on what this guide says. Injuries happen that way.

Difficulty Ratings: All ratings in this guide are subjective. You may have an easier or harder time on a route than the rating suggests. Just because you can climb 12c somewhere else doesn't mean you can climb one here. It may be easier or harder than you expect. Some of Austin's ratings are stiff, others are soft.

Falling Rock: This is limestone, and no matter how much it's climbed on, rocks still fall. Animals at the top of routes have been known to knock down rocks large enough to land you in the hospital. Holds break, rocks trundle, etc. Always be aware!

ACCESS

For the most part, the climbing in Austin is fairly unrestricted. There are a few areas around town, however, that climbing has been closed, and some of those areas contain many of the best routes. This book only contains areas that are open to climbing. When people go to the areas that are closed, it does not bode well for our community, and threatens access to those spots that are currently open.

As always, you should leave no trace. Tread softly where you climb, be polite, keep the area clean, and do whatever you can to ensure that the powers that be allow us to continue to climb on this fantastic rock.

Jade Weaver on an on sight attempt on "Rock Retard"

BOLTING POLICIES

Many of the routes throughout Austin were bolted without approval from any governing body. These days, however, there is a process that must be followed in order for new hardware to be installed on any route except Reimer's (this may change in the future, but for now, there is no approval process at Reimer's Ranch). With so many climbers in such a small area, without such a process, we could quickly loose access to all of our climbing areas.

If you would like to establish a new route in Austin, assuming you can find a square foot of rock that is without a bolt, you must first fill out a bolting application, which you can get at any of the CTM (Central Texas Mountaineers) meetings. Also, a downloadable copy is housed at www.erockonline.com and can be mailed to one of the officers. From there, the application is voted on by the CTM, and then passed on to PARD (Austin Parks and Recreation Department). A waiting period of 60 days must pass without being rejected by PARD for the application to be approved.

If you want to bolt a route, you must follow this process. If you do not, your route will be removed!

The Greenbelt has a Memorandum of Understanding (MOU) that governs how and where new bolts may be added. Please read the following if you are considering bolting a route in the greenbelt:

Central Texas Mountaineers' Zoning Proposal for Climbing in the Austin City Parks Barton Creek Greenbelt Scope and Purpose

This proposal for zoning climbing in the Austin Parks and Recreation Department (PARD) Barton Creek Greenbelt defines a technical climbing management program for climbing areas in the Park and is designed to maintain and enhance technical climbing Barton Springs to Lost Creek. Future zoning proposals shall be implemented as deemed necessary by PARD and the Austin climbing community's representatives, the Central Texas Mountaineers (CTM) and the Central Texas Climbing Committee (CTCC) in agreement with the Memorandum of Cooperation (MOC) between these entities. Previously unclimbed areas or areas currently without fixed protection on the Austin Greenbelt which are brought to the attention of CTM or CTCC will be evaluated for proper designation under the zoning proposal. This current proposal serves as a program for the regulation and maintenance of established climbing areas in the park. This proposal meets the requirements of the MOC between PARD, CTM, and CTCC.

Proposed Zones

Two zoning designations are proposed for the climbing areas on the Austin Greenbelt.

ZONE 1 -- No new fixed protection routes.

This zone prohibits the addition of new fixed protection routes within a designated area (fixed protection includes bolts, pitons, or other permanent hardware). Maintenance and replacement of existing fixed protection, as per the MOC agreement, will be performed within Zone 1 by volunteers of the climbing community under the auspices of CTM and CTCC, and the city will be apprised of such improvement.
Areas to be covered by Zone 1 are the following:

-- Rappeller's Wall
-- The New Wall Area
-- Gus Fruh Area
-- Urban Assault Wall
-- Airman's Cave Wall
-- Sanctuary Wall

Zone 2 -- Application only fixed protection for new routes.

This zone requires that proposed new routes undergo an application process similar to that employed by CTCC and the Texas Parks and Wildlife Department (TPWD) at Enchanted Rock State Park. Proposals for new routes must be written by the person Intending to establish the route and must include a detailed description of the area, the route's location, and how and where fixed protection will

be placed. The proposal should be submitted to CTCC and it will then be reviewed by a joint committee of CTCC and PARD to determine the cultural, environmental, and operations impacts of the new route. Both PARD and CTCC have the authority to approve or reject the application within 60 days of its submission, and those not rejected within that time period will be deemed approved. Areas to be covered by Zone 2 are the following:

-- Wasp Wall upstream to the Balrog Wall (with the understanding that no fixed protection may be placed on top of the Balrog Wall due to private property lines -- i.e., all anchors must be hanging belays)
-- Campbell's Hole Wall
-- Random Walls right of The New Wall Area
-- The 5.8 Wall left of The New Wall Area
-- The Seismic Wall
-- All climbing or potential climbing walls south of Loop 360 Bridge to the Park's boundary at Lost Creek

Conclusion
It is understood that in the future, Zone 2, application areas, may revert to Zone 1, no new fixed protection areas, when PARD in consultation with CTCC and CTM deem them unsuitable for new fixed protection routes.

CLIMATE

It is possible to climb in Austin all year long. Some folks choose to climb at different areas, however, depending on the weather. Texas only has two seasons each year.

March – May:
This is a good time for climbing in Austin. Temperatures are moderate making nearly all destinations enjoyable. Temperatures can range from 75° to 85°.

June – August:
Temperatures are getting hot, and humidity will make chalk turn to mud on many days. Locals are usually not deterred. Pace Bend is a good place to go for deep water soloing. Mosquito's are a nuisance. Temperatures range from 85° to 105°.

September – November:

Temperatures are starting to cool down and climbing is more comfortable in all areas. Temperatures range from 80° to 95°.

December – February:

Climbing is often interrupted by periods of holiday cheer and rain. Temperatures range from just below freezing to about 65°.

Best Hot Day Areas	**Best Cold Day Areas**
1) Sex Cave	1) Seismic
2) Pace Bend	2) New/Great Wall
3) Gus Fruh	3) McKinney Falls

SUGGESTIONS:

Must Do Routes:

5.8   -   Eight Flake (Reimer's)
5.9   -   Tree Route (Reimer's)
             Meet the Flintstones (Greenbelt)
5.10   -   Prototype (Reimer's)
             Diving For Rocks (Greenbelt)
5.11a -   Blowing Smoke at the Monkey (Reimer's)
5.11b -   Hysteria (Greenbelt)
5.11c -   Crankenstein (Reimer's)
5.11d -   Let Them Eat Flake (Reimer's)
5.12a -   Tunnel Vision (Greenbelt)
5.12b -   Stranglehold (Reimer's)
5.12c -   Catharsis Roof (Reimer's)
5.12d -   Bolus (Reimer's)
5.13a -   Block Party (Reimer's)
5.13b -   Lucky Strikes (Reimer's)
5.13c -   Wild Spider (Reimer's)
5.13d -   Irreverent Youth (Reimer's)

Free Soloist

People enjoy this sort of thing, and some have lived long enough to tell tall tales about it. Austin is full of Limestone, and even the best holds can break off. Imagine the surprise of the person who pulled the key hold off "Through the Looking Glass". If you are one who likes to get high on the rock sans rope, be warned. The rock can and does break.

Camping

The Greenbelt and Reimer's do not allow camping. If you try to camp at Reimer's, they will personally throw you out. Don't do it. If you camp in the Greenbelt, you could get a ticket from the city. There is fee camping at Pace Bend and McKinney.

Pets

There are leash laws almost everywhere. It is recommended that you keep your dog on a leash because when dogs start fighting, people start yelling, and climbers start falling. Oh, and don't let your dog crap on the trail.

Water and Food

Climbing in Austin allows for an escape from the urban world, but at the same time allows for the comforts that come with the city. Convenience stores and restaurants are everywhere, and water is easy to find. Be sure to bring water with you to the climbing areas, as potable water is not "on tap" at any of the climbing areas.

Barton Creek Greenbelt

Valeria Camnasio on "Cedar Fever". Photo by Tim Stich

Barton Creek Greenbelt - Overview

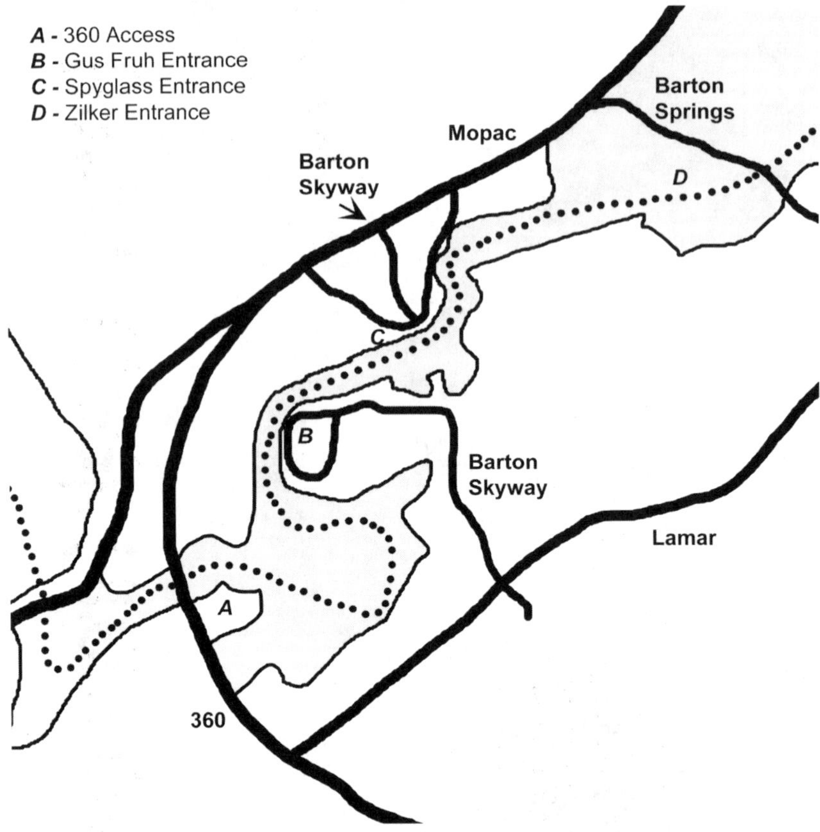

360 Access

From Mopac (Loop 1) head south towards 360 (Capital of TX. Hwy) and exit 360 West (the exit is from the far left lane). Continue to the stop light and turn left into the business center and turn left immediately at the parking lot. Park in the gravel parking lot at the Barton Creek access trail. Hike down the trail and around the bike restriction fence. You will see the tall wall across the creek (usually dry). When the creek is full and rapid, approach by hiking across the bridge and skirting down the scree on the wall side of the creek.

Seismic Wall (Maggy's Wall) (from right to left)

This is a fantastic wall that is well bolted and well traveled. No route is harder than about 11c (except for one) and allows the beginning climber to get their feet wet with a wide array of climbs all in one spot. A rack of 3 to 5 quick draws and a couple long ones for the anchors is about all you need here. This wall has the fastest approach in the greenbelt (when the creek is dry). The unique orange coloration of the wall is quite interesting as well.

History of Maggy:

"Born in Kansas, Maggy moved to Austin in the early eighties. She spent most of her youth developing the skills that would serve her so well as she matured. The games of Frisbee developed the eye mouth coordination that was needed when she began **diving for rocks**, sometimes at depths of 3' – 4' under water. The crude raiding of only the most bountiful trash cans nurtured the ability used in later years to open refrigerators or to acquire, from strangers, complete boxes of chicken with side orders and condiments. This type of activity gave rise to her nickname **Hoover Head**. For like the Hoover vacuum cleaner, her **hoovering** of whatever hit the floor was absolute.

She became a **rock dog** after an experience that changed her life. It was on her first trip to Enchanted Rock that she played the part of a typical tour-on without taking adequate precaution. She climbed the main dome in the middle of summer. The heat of the granite literally burned the pads off her feet. After months of convalescing she was determined to return. This time she was ready. Realizing she **needs new shoes** for the hot sharp granite crystals of E-rock, she donned leather boots designed especially for her. With her blue back pack full of water, bones and chow she was there to drive the dome.

Once hooked by this sport she toured to all of the local crags: Gus Fruh, New Wall, Reimer's, and Sunken Gardens. But her true love was the road trips to Hueco, New Mexico, Colorado, and Arizona, for it was on these trips that she could bark nonstop for up to 10 hours at a time. When stuck in the back of a truck she would **lick the window** that divides the camper shell from the cab trying to get into the cab. When riding in the cab, she would put her nose right next to the windshield, thereby assuring her position as the leader of the pack. Unfortunately quick stops left many **nose prints on the windshield.** While the barking did not always make her the most endearing road companion, she always displayed proper decorum upon arriving at her destination. She was always welcome at the most chic boarding houses from the Sheraton in Denver to the Sioux Inn at Post.

She was a great climbing companion. Her warm up for climbs consisted of retrieving anything that was available. When satisfied with her efforts, she would sit down and eat whatever she had in front of her. Be it wood or be it stone, she chewed to heart's delight. Some of the items were a little hard to swallow and she would have to **ACK** them out of her throat. When it was time to get on the rock she became focused waiting and watching at the bottom of the climb until the descent was complete she could not be distracted, except for maybe a **butt scratch**. And upon the return of her climbing partners she would get so excited that she would not just wag her tail, but also her whole body. This body wag was known as **just a wiggle butt.**

Late in life Maggy took on a roommate, **Roo Dog**. While Roo Dog had the great go-for-it attitude, she was a little stiff and sometimes looked more like a **torpedo** than a black lab. The two of them got along great, Roo Dog was **Maggy's Best Friend**. They shared a common bond in their desire for **ice cubes, popcorn, and popsicles,** the only human foods they were given to eat.

We put up these routes in her memory during the winter of 1993. We hope you enjoy the climbing as much as we loved **The Magster."**

Chris Campbell, Bruce Decker, and Tom Suhler.

1) Hollywood (5.6 TR)

On the far right side of the wall is a low angle dihedral with TR anchors. To set a TR climb "Roo Dog" and traverse right to drop a line. (FA – Ralph Showalter)

2) Roo Dog (AKA "Maggy's Best Friend") (5.8)

This route seems harder than the rating permits because of the polished nature of the rock. There is a decent distance between bolts by greenbelt standards, but there are large ledges between bolts from which to clip. (3 bolts, 2 top anchors with chains) (FA – Tom Suhler, Bruce Becker)

3) Butt Scratch (5.8)

Follow polished climbing past big ledges and fun edges. This route used to go left after the 3rd bolt to the 4th bolt of "Wiggle". Since this route has been given its own anchors though, it goes up and right after the third bolt to the anchors. (3 bolts, 2 top anchors with links) (FA – Tom Suhler, Bruce Becker)

4) It's a Wiggle Butt (5.8+)*

Use small crimps and smears to the second bolt, and past big ledges to the third bolt. The crux is figuring out how to maneuver the polished rock to the 4th bolt. (4 bolts, 2 top anchors with chains) (FA – Tom Suhler, Bruce Becker)

5) Over Easy (5.9) **

Clip the first bolt then move left and up to a small roof above. Pull the roof and move right to find the anchors. (5 bolts, 2 top anchors with chains)

6) Over Easy Direct (5.9+) **

Instead of clipping the first bolt and moving left, start directly under the second bolt and make the thin sequence to gain the second bolt. Continue as with "Over Easy".

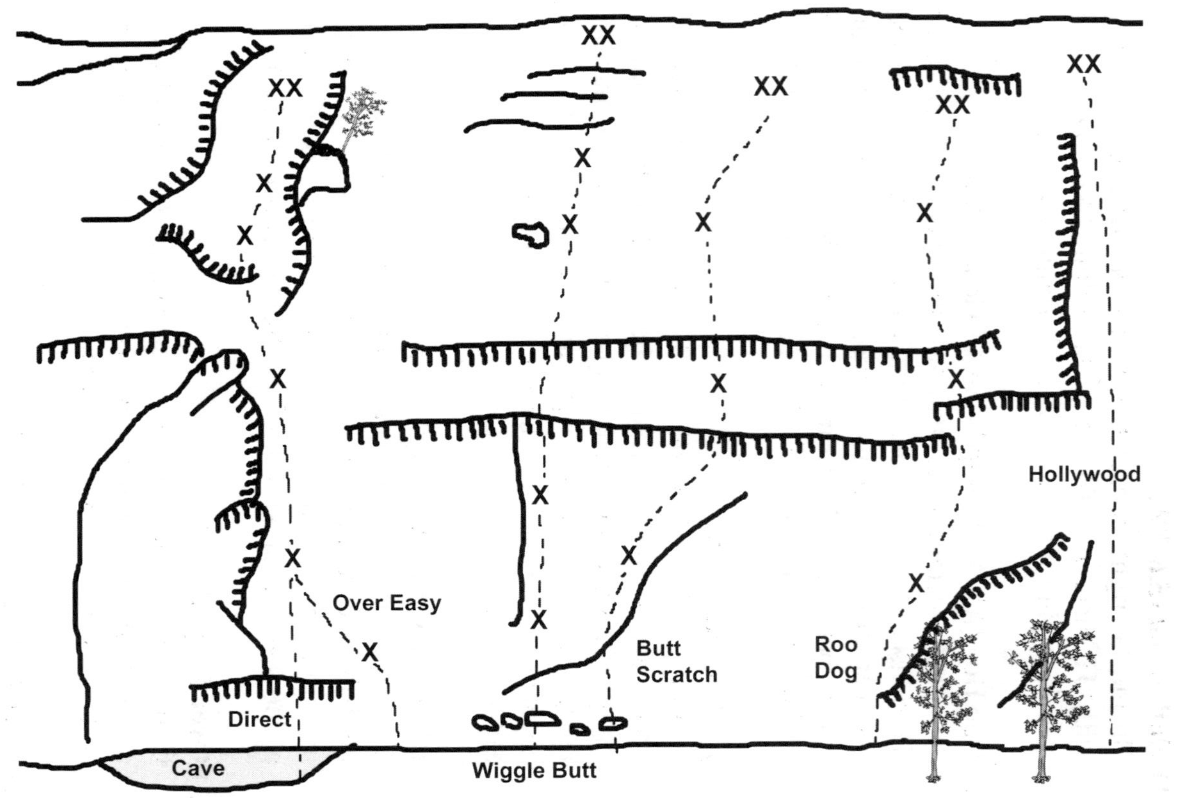

AustinRock
ErockOnline.com

Evan Jackson on "Over Easy". Photo: John Beveridge

7) Maggy Needs New Shoes (5.9 TR)*

This is the direct line under the anchors for "Ice Cubes". (FA – Tom Suhler, Bruce Becker)

8) Ice Cubes, Popcorn, and Popsicles (5.10-)

Denoted by the wide crack midway up the wall. Affectionately known as "Slimy Crack". (3 bolts, 2 top anchors with chains) (FA – Tom Suhler, Bruce Becker)

9) Diving For Rocks (5.10d)***

This is the middle route under the roof. (4 bolts, 2 top anchors with chains) (FA – Tom Suhler, Bruce Becker)

10) Lonesome Dove (5.12)***

From the anchors of "Diving", keep going through the roof. (1 bolt in roof, 2 cold shut anchors over lip)

Evan Jackson on "Lonesome Dove". Photo: John Beveridge

AustinRock
ErockOnline.com

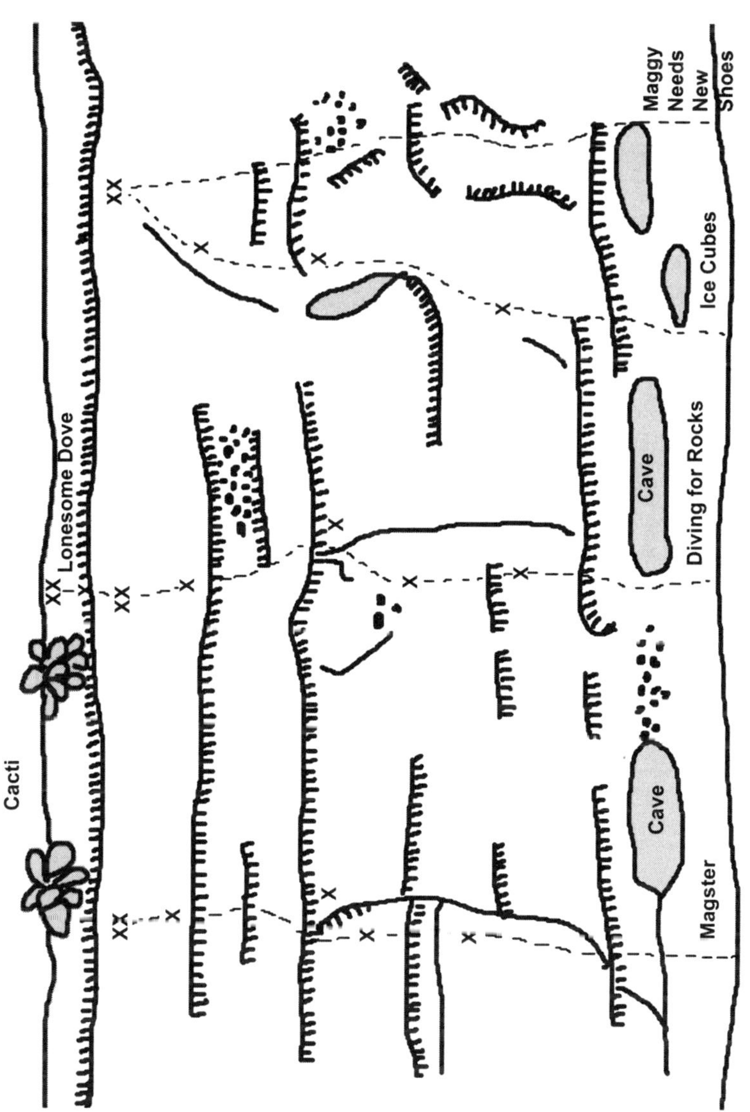

Maggy Needs New Shoes
Ice Cubes
Cave
Diving for Rocks
Cave
Magster
Lonesome Dove
Cacti

11) Magster (5.10a)**

A one move wonder, but is well worth the effort. The layback is very fun. Follow big ledges to the anchors past the crux. There is an old, original bolt above the anchors without a hanger. (4 bolts, 2 top anchors with chains) (FA – Tom Suhler, Bruce Becker)

12) Rock Dog (5.10+)

This route originally had two bolts and a two bolt anchor. Now, there is just one bolt about 20 feet up just left of the little branch on the bulge. (FA – Tom Suhler, Bruce Becker)

13) Nose Print on the Windshield (5.11c) ***

The hardest, yet shortest route at Seismic. Start off the semi-detached portion of rock to gain the first bolt. Don't use the crack to the right to get the full effect. (Use the crack and the route becomes 11a) To make this route more interesting, make one extra move past the anchors and clip them at your knees. (3 bolts, 2 top anchors with chains) (FA – Tom Suhler, Bruce Becker)

14) She's No Dog; She's My Wife (5.11b) ***

This is a great route, with interesting moves right off the deck. Stick clip the first bolt to avoid a digger if you mess up on the opening moves. (4 bolts, 2 top anchors with chains) (FA – Tom Suhler, Bruce Becker)

15) ACK! (5.11b)

The beginning of this route is seriously contrived since staying out of "Seismic Step" is very difficult. The top is quite fun though. (4 bolts, 2 top anchors with chains) (FA – Tom Suhler, Bruce Becker)

16) Seismic Step (5.8 TR)

Follow the obvious low angle dihedral between "Ack" and "Lick". There are TR anchors. (FA – Keith Guillory)

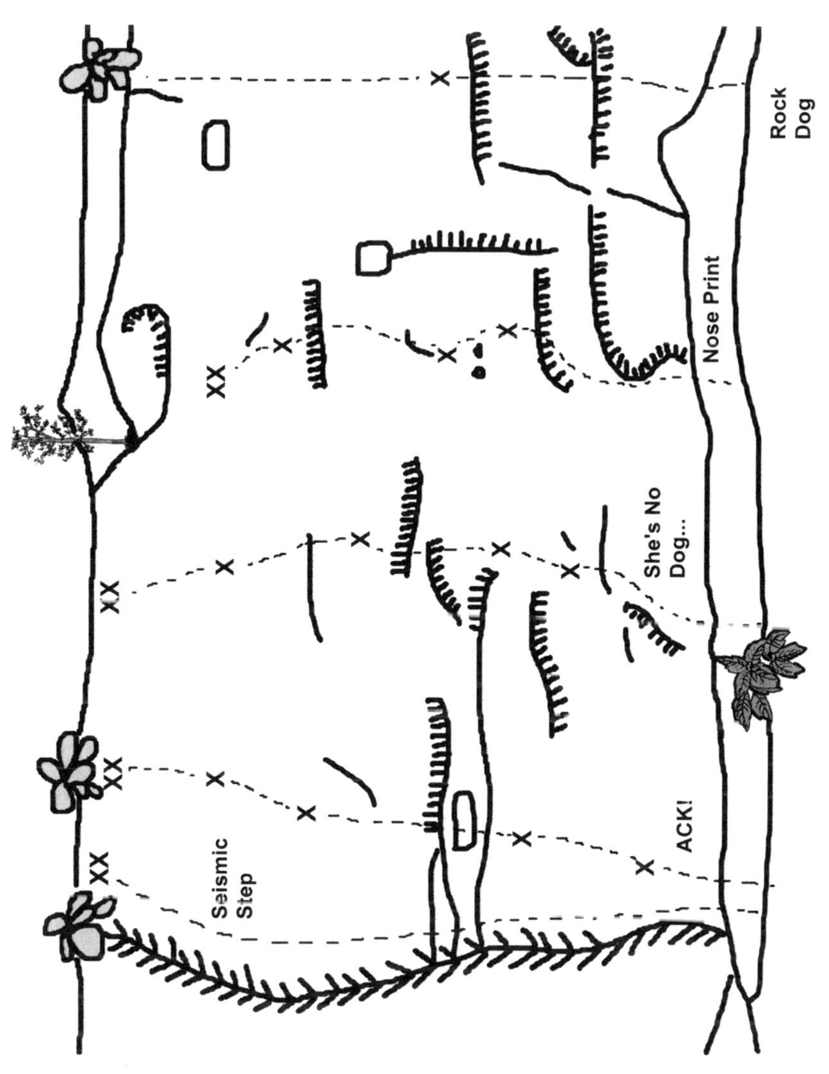

Rock Dog
Nose Print
She's No Dog....
ACK!
Seismic Step

17) Lick the Window (5.10)***

The first bolt is now very high since the flood in early 2003 removed a large bolder from the start. Make an interesting move right off the deck to gain the first bolt past a good ledge. Follow fun climbing straight up to the anchors. (3 bolts, 2 top anchors with chains) (FA – Tom Suhler, Bruce Becker)

18) Matter of Honor (5.10)*

This route is immediately left of "Lick the Window". Make a tenuous move off a right hand crimp to a good pocket by the first bolt. Move right through a couple more strong moves to the second bolt. Above the second bolt the route is basically over. (3 bolts, 2 top anchors)

19) Angel of Poets (5.10a)*

This is another new route between "Matter of Honor" and the deep, arm sized hole in the wall. The first few moves are where the fun is at, and after the second bolt, it's all over. (3 bolts, 2 top anchors)

20) Torpedo (5.11 TR)

At one time there were probably TR anchors for this route but no longer. Locate this never climbed route somewhere between "Angel" and "Hoovering". Good Luck! (FA – Tom Suhler, Bruce Becker)

21) Hoovering (5.9 TR)

Ten feet left of "Angel of Poets" and just right of "Hoover Head" is this TR. Climb the direct line to the anchors of "Hoover Head". (FA – Tom Suhler, Bruce Becker)

Hire a qualified guide to this area at Rock-About.com

AustinRock
ErockOnline.com

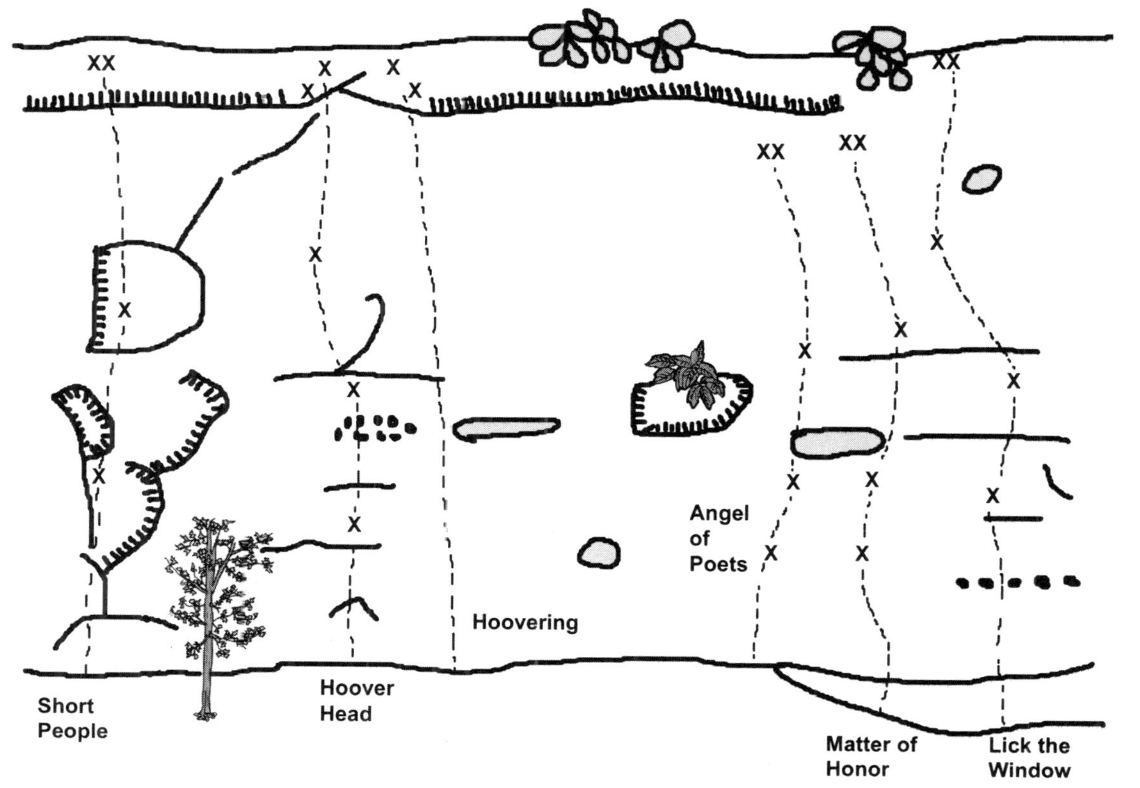

Short
People
Hoover
Head
Hoovering
Angel
of
Poets
Matter of
Honor
Lick the
Window

22) Hoover Head (5.9)**

Just to the right of the trees is this route. The crux is at the top getting to the anchors. The anchors are very wide, but below each chain is an extra bolt with a link on it. This is so you can TR "Hoovering". (3 bolts, 2 top anchors with chains) (FA – Tom Suhler, Bruce Becker)

23) Short People (5.9)

Start just to the left of the trees that grow from the base of the wall. This route will make you think. (2 bolts, 2 top anchors with chains)

24) The Sneak (V?)

This is a boulder problem located 75 yards upstream, towards the bridge. A 50 foot traverse with hands from 3 – 7 feet off the ground. ("The Sneak was Maggy's way of starting at the foot of the bed and slowly moving to the middle. Once there she would try to convince you that you would be much more comfortable sleeping on the couch and letting her have the entire bed").

On the left side of the wall, well left of the "Short People" are several high ball boulder problems. On the right side of Seismic Wall are several shorter boulder problems. It's worth the time to explore these small intricacies as it is good rock that gets very little attention.

Beehive Wall (Left to Right)

To approach Beehive Wall, park at the 360 Access just as with Seismic Wall. Once at the trail, turn left and hike under the 360 bridge. The walls start about a half mile down the trail, after you pass the wooden bridge. There are seven routes, starting immediately after you pass the chain bolted to the wall. Notice the other-worldly huge beehive high on the wall. There are several obscurities to the left and right of the main Beehive Wall.

1) Meat and Potatoes (5.10a)

Find this route as you are approaching the Beehive Wall. It is a crack climb that is somewhat obvious about 100 yards downstream from Beehive Wall. It's a trad only route with no anchors. The crux comes at the top and is usually dirty.

2) Sucker Sipper (5.11)

30 feet downstream from the chain bolted to the wall at Beehive is this route. The first bolt is above a pine tree on a ledge. Climb through 5.7 moves to a thin, balance 5.11 sequence at the top. The route has no anchors, but currently has an old wad of webbing with a ring slung around a cedar tree. (3 bolts) (FA- Mark Pell, Alvino Pon)

3) Honey Dripper (5.11c)

This route looks like it would be the most fun on the wall, but the bee's have claimed it as their own. Finish to an alternate set of bolts out left for an easier finish called **Big Dipper (5.11a)**. (8 bolts, 2 top anchors)(FA – Kirk Holliday, Alvino Pon)

4) Dirty Rotten Whore (5.12a)

To the right of the hive is a line with two variations. Go straight up or go left at the 5th bolt to another set of anchors called **Prickly Heat**. (7 bolts, 2 top anchors) (FA – Alvino Pon)

5) Champagne n' Reefer (5.12d)

This route has Eye Bolts. (7 bolts, 2 top anchors w/ chains)

6) Super Yummy (5.12 c/d)

Start on the right side of the cave on top of the block. Manufactured holds through the roof, and some of them have broken off. The crux comes right off the deck and then eases slightly above. (6 bolts, 2 bolt anchor)

7) Hedonistic Urges (5.12a/b)

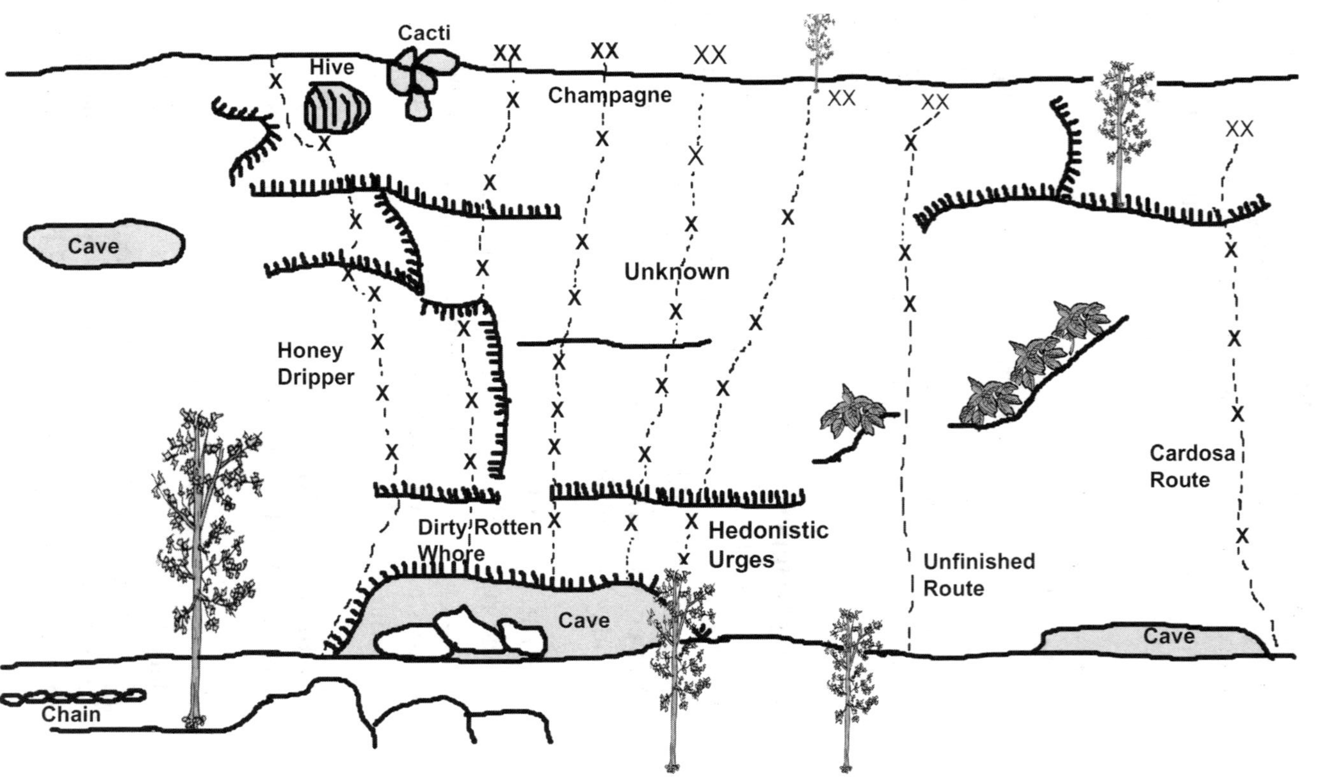

Cacti
Hive
Champagne
Cave
Unknown
Honey Dripper
Dirty Rotten Whore
Hedonistic Urges
Cave
Cardosa Route
Unfinished Route
Cave
Chain

8) Unfinished Route (5.?)

This route has three bolts up high on the wall, and may likely never be completed. The FA information is unknown.

9) Cardosa Route (5.10) **

This is the last route on this wall. The first bolt is high and is best clipped with a stick clip. The exciting moves are at the beginning and the end of the route. There is a hanger-less bolt above the first bolt, but is not included in the bolt count. This was the first route to go in on this wall. (4 bolts, 2 top anchors with rap links)

On the right side of Beehive Wall is long traverse that follows several sections of increasingly vague holds. If the bees are too bad on the wall, this might make for some fun climbing in a quiet area as not many climbers visit.

Under Mopac Bridge

Under the North bound side of the Mopac Bridge at Hwy 360 is a tall aid route. From Hwy 360 at Mopac, head south on the Frontage road but do not enter southbound Mopac traffic. Instead, stay on the service road as it begins to loop back around under the Mopac Bridge. Park here. Hike down to the second abutment on the North side. On the backside of this structure is this aid route with bolts sticking out of the wall and a couple drilled pockets up high.

Urban Surprise (C0)***

This was originally a free climb that was installed by Greg Brooks in the early 90's called "Killer Pillar". The Austin Bridge People found it and took all of the holds down. They left the bolts sticking out which now makes for a fantastic aid line. (FAA – Sean O'Grady)

5.8 Sanctuary (left to right)

To approach the 5.8 Sanctuary, use the 360 Access just as with the Seismic Wall and Beehive Wall. The 5.8 Sanctuary is about a quarter mile downstream (North) from Seismic on the same side of the creek. If the water is high, hike across the bridge and approach from the wall side of the creek. Otherwise, you can hike down the trail on either side to get there.

This is a quaint little area, with only a couple notable routes to mention. The rock quality is superb, and the huge hueco's in the wall are an interesting feature. This short wall is only about 25 feet high, and is worth visiting, if only once. The names given here may or may not be what the first ascensionist had in mind.

1) Fist Crack (5.7)*

Climb the obvious crack in the dihedral. There are a couple great jams up high. Even though this is a crack, there are many face holds that one can use to ascend this short delight. This crack can be climbed using large gear for pro, or set a TR off the anchors for "Face Off".

2) Face Off (5.9)**

This route is in the middle of the wall directly over the cave. Clip the first bolt then gain the face until you can reach the second bolt. The rock quality is fantastic. Too bad this route is so short. (2 bolts, 2 top anchors w/ rap links)

3) Face On (5.10)**

This very contrived route is the same as "Face Off" but tends to climb the left side of the bolts. Do a hard pull over the cave to gain the face and use small holds to the left of "Face Off".

4) Swordfish (5.8 TR)*

Just to the right of the bolt line for "Face Off" are two shallow finger cracks that allow for the occasional jam. The rock is great, and the climbing fun, but short. Set TR off "Face Off".

5) Pointless Wonder (5.4)

Around the corner right of the main wall, one can find a small crack in a dihedral that allows for decent finger jams. The angle is soft, and the climb is short. Possibly a good beginner trad climb, although taking a fall may or may not mean hitting the ground. There are no anchors above.

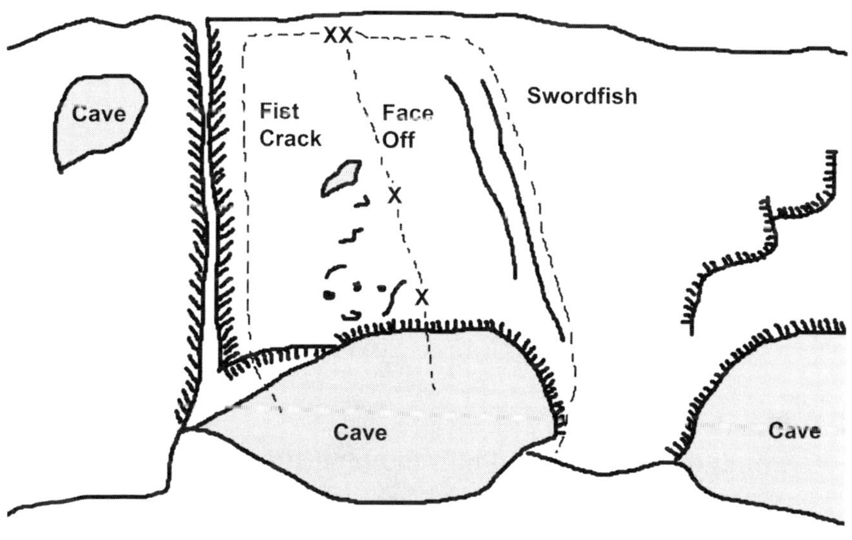

Kirk and Alvin's Wall

Kirk and Alvin's Wall is approached from the 360 Access just as the other walls in this area. Hike downstream (North) on the main trail until it crosses the creek bed (a little more than a quarter mile). Before you cross over to the other side of the creek, veer right and hike along the creek following a faint trail in the general direction of the rock wall ahead. Continue hiking for approximately a quarter mile more until you see a trail leading up to the rock face. The first thing you will likely see is the entrance to Airman's Cave. Turn left and follow the path to the base of these climbs.

The rock quality at Kirk and Alvin's Wall is questionable in some areas. Because of the inactivity here, nearly every hold is dirty, and many are brittle. It's not uncommon to grab a flake and wonder if it will hold your weight. The routes are good, they just need to be climbed more. It is recommended that if you climb here, you and your belayer wear a helmet.

1) **Bloody Butt (5.9+)**
   On the left side of the wall you will find a low first bolt to the left of the obvious crack. Rock quality is poor until you pass the second bolt. Climb straight up past a third bolt to the closely spaced anchors above. (3 bolts, 2 top anchors w/ chains)(FA – Kirk Holladay, Alvino Pon)

2) **Skank Hole (5.9+)**
   Climb to the ledge and clip the high first bolt. From here move left into the crack and go straight up to the second bolt above. (For a harder variation, go straight up over the bulge after the first bolt instead of moving left into the crack). Follow holds that may or may not be there directly up and then move right to the anchors. (2 bolts, 2 top anchors) (FA – Kirk Holladay, Alvino Pon)

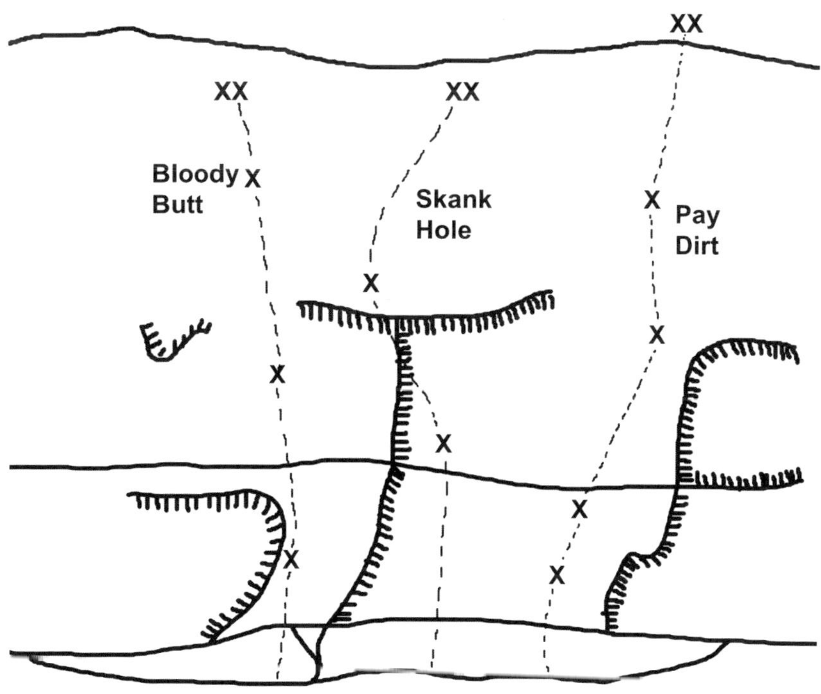

3) Pay Dirt (5.10c)*

On the right side of the face is this well protected route. Clip the first two bolts then make the challenging move over the bulge following a hollow flake. Find a great rest at the third bolt. The anchors are set way back. (4 bolts, 2 top anchors) (FA – Kirk Holladay, Alvino Pon)

4) X-Rated Negro (5.10 TR)

Set top ropes using trees at the top about 20 feet right of "Pay Dirt". This route climbs the overhanging face with sections of good rock. (FA – Jeff Jackson)

Gus Fruh (left to right)

From Ben White (Hwy 71) exit Lamar and head towards downtown. After about a mile and a half, turn left on Barton Skyway. Drive all the way down to the dead-end (by the church) and turn left on Barton Hills Dr. The entrance for Gus Fruh will be on the right after a mile or so. Hike down the gravel trail staying left at the first split. Cross the creek bed to the trail on the other side, turn right and hike the short distance to the wall. If the creek is high (and rapid), it's safest to approach from the Spyglass entrance and hike the two miles in to Gus Fruh. Many routes were put in on lead.

1) Running Man (5.12a)
Usually wet, with manufactured pockets through the second bolt. You'll have to climb through bushes to a bolt or two. (5 bolts)(FA – Scott Harris, David Cardosa)

2) Reefer Madness (5.11c)**
Follow easy climbing to a high first bolt off the ledge. The lower half of the route is not much harder than 5.10. The crux comes at the top. Find a three finger drilled pocket below the roof. The slabby section over the lip is usually dirty, so your belayer should be aware of potential falling debris. Use long runners to set TR to reduce rope drag.

3) Cyborg (5.11b)**
Start as with "Reefer", but go right after clipping the first bolt. The drag when TR'ing is substantial. Use long runners. (4 bolts, 2 top anchors)(FA – Scott Harris)

4) Birdland (5.10d)**
On the right side of the ledge, clip the high first bolt and make the move over the roof and through the tree limbs. Est.: Fall 1987. (4 bolts, 2 top anchors) (FA – Jeff Jackson)

5) Iranian Arms Deal (5.10d)**

This route starts with a powerful move to gain the ledge
then follows large holds all the way to the anchors. Est.:
Fall 1987. (4 bolts, 2 top anchors)(FA – Keith Guillory,
David Renburg)

6) Fern Bar (5.9)***

Make a tough move to gain the huge ledge above the first
bolt. Clip the piton out right and move up through usually
muddy holds to gain the next bolt. Jug haul to the next
bolt. A hard move at the end will see you over the ledge to
the anchors. (4 bolts, 2 top anchors)(FA – Keith Guillory)

Sean Woods on "Fern Bar"

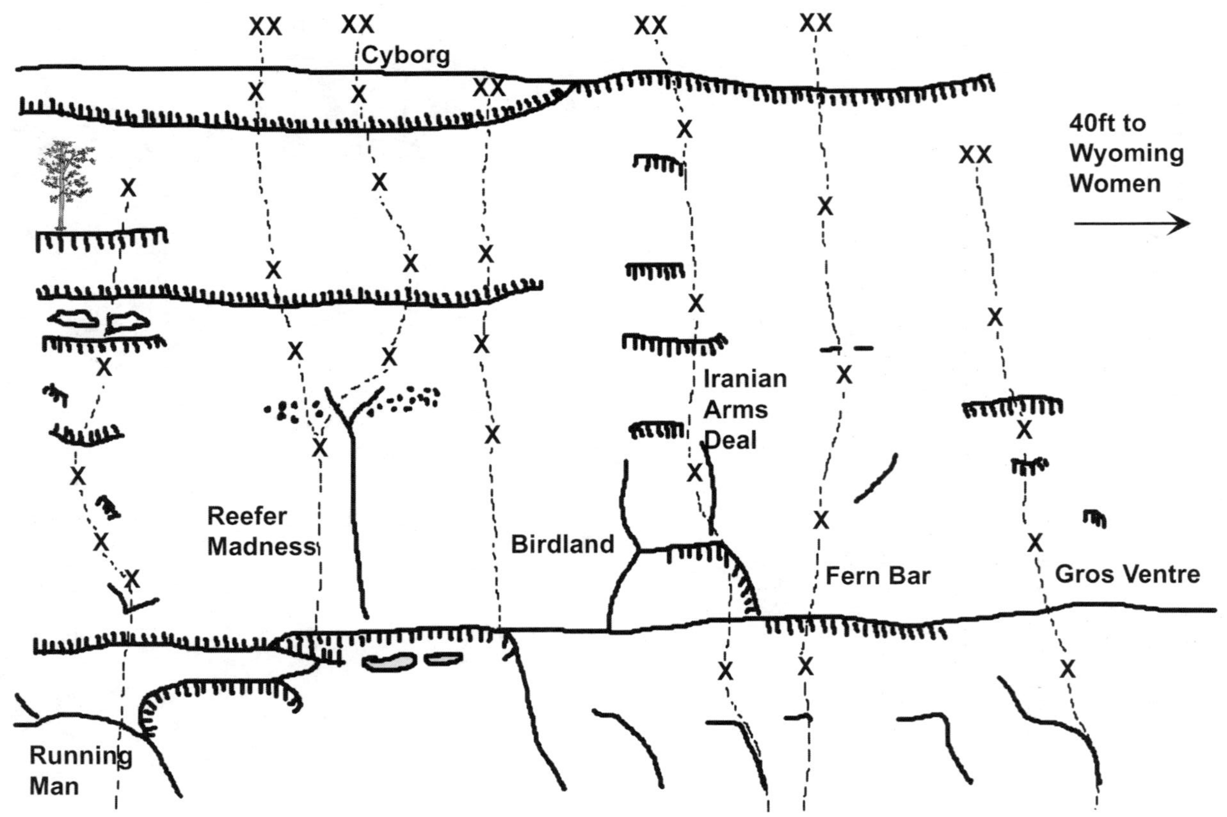

Cyborg
40ft to
Wyoming
Women
Iranian
Arms
Deal
Reefer
Madness
Birdland
Fern Bar
Gros Ventre
Running
Man

7) Gros Ventre (5.11a)***

Clip the first bolt from two nice pockets. Pull hard on the side-pull to gain a rest. Clip the second bolt and make another nice move to gain another rest stance. Clip the third bolt and cruise through 5.8+ climbing past one more bolt and the anchors. (4 bolts, 2 top anchors w/ chains) (FA – David Cardosa)

Tommy Blackwell on "Gros Ventre"

8) Wyoming Women (5.8)

This is the obvious wide crack in the middle of the Gus Fruh wall. There are a couple places where a good hand jam can be found, but the crack is pretty wide otherwise. It is feasible to lead this route with gear, but due to limestone's soft nature, a safer method would be to set top ropes off "Heir Apparent". (FA – George Hazzard)

9) Heir Apparent (5.9)**

A couple feet to the right of "Wyoming Women" is this fun line. Clip the first bolt then make the crux move over the bulge. Good rock and neat moves all the way to the anchors, which are set far back. (4 bolts, 2 top anchors)

10) Chicken Supreme (5.10b TR)

Start to the right of the bulge and follow thin moves to the layback above. One bolt TR. Difficult to set, but can be done from the anchors of "Rock Retard".

11) Betwixt (5.11b)

5 feet right of "Chicken Supreme" on a thin vertical seam. Mantle the roof and finish up the middle to the "Chicken Supreme" anchor. (FA – Ralph Showalter)

12) Egg Salad Sandwich (5.10a)

(AKA Old #9) Start 10 feet right of "Chicken Supreme" and pull the right side of the roof and finish to the right of the bulge to the "Chicken Supreme" anchor.

13) Trash Can Man (5.11a)

Pull the shallow dihedral left of the first bolt. Finish on "Rock Retard". This was the first 5.11 established at Gus Fruh in the spring of 1987. (FA – Hank Caylor)

14) Rock Retard (5.11a)***

A must do route on this wall. The first bolt is below the first roof. Make a hard move to an obvious side-pull and stand up. Move left to clip the third bolt and then make another hard move over the roof. Jug haul to the anchors by the tree. Est.: Spring 1987. (4 bolts, 2 top anchors)(FA – Scott Harris, Randy Spears, Mike Head)

Tommy Blackwell crankin' on "Rock Retard"

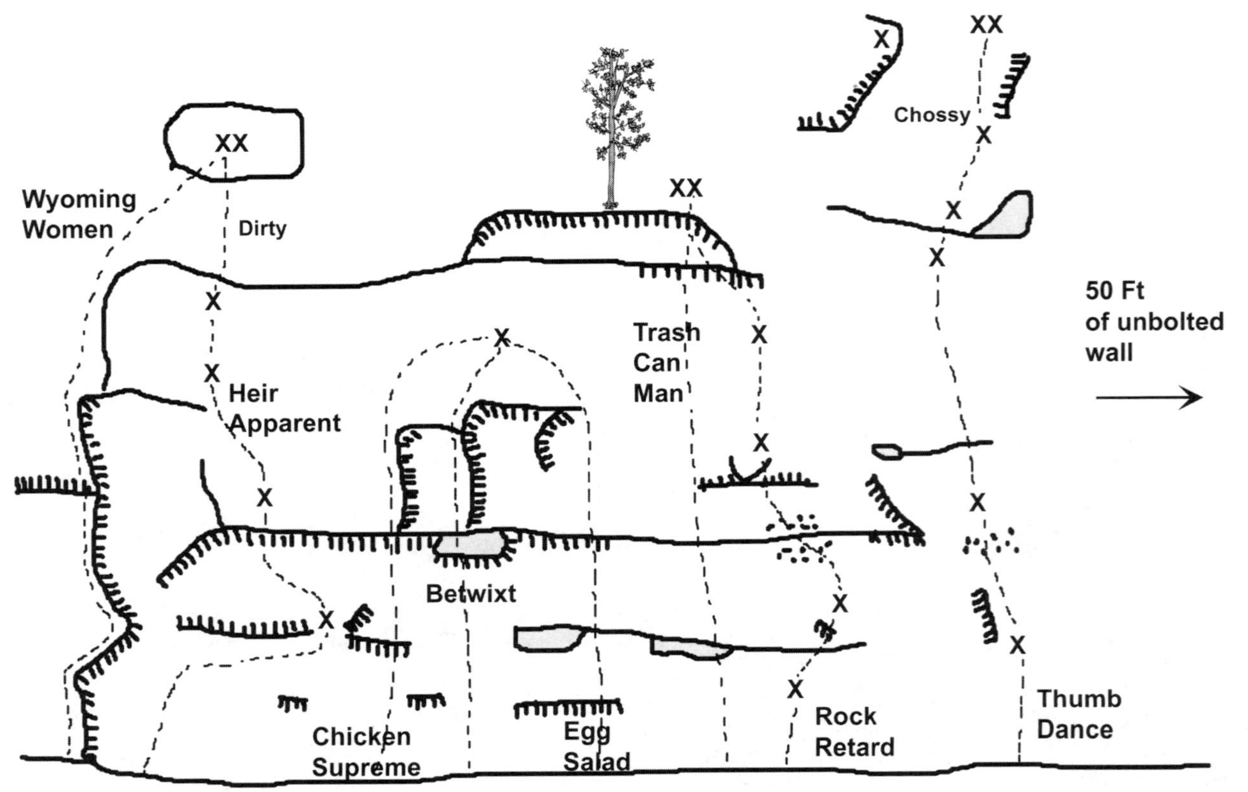

AustinRock
ErockOnline.com

15) Apostrophe (5.11)

Top rope from "Rock Retard". Start right of "Rock Retard" up to two obvious dishes. Bring the feet up high and reach high right to a nice side-pull. Reach the ledge and move through jugs to another face sequence above. Climb left back to the anchor point. (FA – Rick Watson)

16) Thumb Dance (5.10b R)***

Run out between second and third bolts. Major rock fall from the top has made this route a little crumbly, but it is still a great route. (3 pitons, 3 bolts, 2 top anchors) (FA – John Sanders)

17) Blind Date (5.10c)

Start 2 ft right of "Thumb Dance". Go straight up and pull a small roof to the "Thumb Dance" anchors. Use "Thumb Dance" anchors. Est.: Fall 1987. (FA – David Cardosa)

18) Praying Mantel (5.11a)

Five feet right of "Thumb Dance". Follow a dihedral to the right to mantle over the roof. (FA – Ralph Showalter)

19) Wandering Women (5.8)

Start "Wyoming Women", traverse right over a prominent block to the bolt on "Chicken Supreme", and finish "Thumb Dance".

20) Rent a Pig (5.10)

This climb is marked by a bolt sans hanger that sits all alone to the right of "Praying Mantle". There are no other bolts, and there are no anchors. (FA – Ralph Showalter)

21) The Big Traverse (V3)***

This is a great warm-up and allows for over 400 feet of continuous movement. Start on the far left at "Reefer Madness" and move right through two or three cruxes all the way to the cave at Kingdom of Ging. For a full body pump start moving back left once you finish.

22) Green Mile Traverse (V5)***
About 50 yards left of "Running Man" is a short traverse with a noticeable crux. Traverse from right to left, and for the really strong, reverse the whole thing.

The Whipping Post Boulder

The Whipping Post Boulder is close to the creek bed directly in front of "Thumb Dance". There are supposedly about 30 problems on this boulder, but not many names or beta are known. There are a couple notable problems that are well worth the time to unlock the sequence. As for the rest of the boulder, a good imagination and a crash pad will enable you to stay entertained for days.

1) Secret Sharer (V4)**
Found on the short, vertical face opposite the creek bed (facing "Thumb Dance"). Sit start and locate the hidden left foot on the under side of the boulder (the secret) and dyno to a small crimp high on the face. Top out. (FA – Adam Metzger)

2) Whipping Post (V5)***
This problem climbs the roof of the boulder. Start sitting on the sloping hand rail and make the lunge to an open hold in the roof. Get a good heel hook and reach over the roof to a small but good crimp. The top out involves a couple one-arm pull ups since you have no feet.

Kingdom of Ging (left to right)

The Kingdom of Ging is the short section of wall to the right of the main Gus Fruh Wall with the huge cave below the start of all the routes. There are several nice bouldering opportunities under the roof here too, with most problems in the V4 and V5 range.

1) Charlie Don't Surf (5.10d)***
This is the left most route that starts under the roof below the broken tufa. Jump start to the ledge then move through nice crimpers to the third bolt. For a nice rest, move slightly left from the third bolt to relax before clipping the fourth bolt, otherwise move straight in to begin the crux early. Est.: Fall 1987. (4 bolts, 2 top anchors/ chains) (FA – Scott Harris, David Cardosa)

2) Jerry's Kids (5.11b)***
Make the difficult mantle over the cave and clip the high first bolt. Follow 5.9 climbing past the second bolt to a rest under the bulge. Move up to the crimpers and move right to set up for the sloper above (crux move). Climb up the flake and reach the anchors by the tree. Est.: Spring 1987. (5 bolts, 2 top anchors w/ chains) (FA – Mike Head, Scott Harris, Randy Spears)

3) Sex Dwarf's (5.11c)
Start "King of Ging" but instead of moving straight up to the fourth bolt, go left to the bolt on the bulge then straight up to the bolt under the cave and on to the anchors. (FA – Steve Languell)

4) King of Ging (5.10b) **

This was the first route on this wall. Jump start to the ledge on the right side of the cave and mantle over to reach the first bolt. Climb through large holds to the third bolt then continue straight up to the fourth bolt. From here reach the lip of the cave above and traverse right to the last bolt. The anchors are directly above. Est.: Fall 1986. (5 bolts, 2 top anchors/ chains) (FA – Hank Caylor)

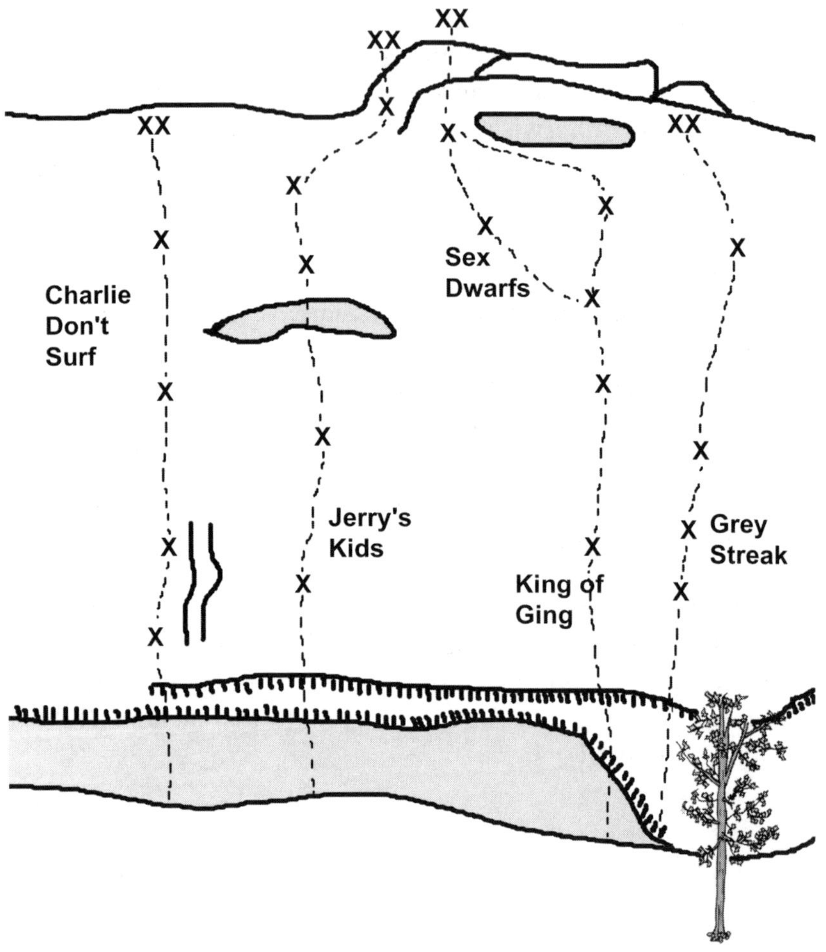

5) Grey Streak (5.10b) **

Start off the triangle boulder below the ledge and mantle over to reach the first bolt. There are three closely spaced bolts at the bottom, but the crux comes at the fourth bolt above. The anchors are below the small roof above. One anchor is a rap link. (4 bolts, 2 top anchors) (FA – Tony Faucett)

Guide's Wall (left to right)

The Guides Wall is the next section of wall to the right of the Kingdom of Ging in the Gus Fruh area. The wall is often used by climbing guides and other groups to teach climbing skills. There are various bolts up top to set top ropes. Generally it's a good idea to have long slings in order to set up a TR properly. A relatively easy approach can be found on either the left or right side of the wall.

1) Bulge (5.9)

Climb over the noticeable bulge on the left side of the wall. (FA – John Sanders)

2) Thin Crack (5.5)

Below the bulge on the right side are two parallel seams, one a bit wider than the other. This is the crack on the left, which will just take fingers. (FA – John Sanders, Lauren Clayton)

3) Stand Off (5.9)

Climb the thin seam immediately right of "Thin Crack". (FA – Ralph Showalter)

4) Flash Crack (5.6)

A nice under-cling crack marks the beginning of this route. Follow the broken rock up to the gully above and top out. (FA John Sanders, Lauren Clayton)

5) April Fool (5.9)***

Towards the right side of the wall is a long seam that runs almost all the way to the top. Scramble up to the seam and let the fun begin. (FA – Ralph Showalter)

6) Touch of Class (5.7)

This is the wide crack on the right side of the wall. (FA – John Sanders)

7) Steep Bulge (5.10)

Start just as with "Touch of Class" but leave the comfort of the crack and climb the direct line to the anchor point.

8) Guides Wall Traverse (V2+)

The grade stays about the same whether you traverse left to right or right to left.

Urban Assault (left to right)

To get to the Urban Assault Wall, use the Gus Fruh Access and instead of turning right as with Gus Fruh, turn left and hike for about one half mile. The trail is better on the far side of the creek, but if the water is high, you can follow a decent, but less traveled trail on the entrance side of the creek. The large wall will be easily seen on your left. The Urban Assault wall is the largest wall in the Greenbelt at about 90 feet tall, but is also one of the crumbliest. This area is rarely visited as the routes are very suspect. If you choose to climb here, be mindful of the gear you're clipping into, as it may be good, but the rock around it not. It's not uncommon for entire ledges the size of suitcases to come off when weighted. Climbing here is like climbing inside a furnace, as the wall faces the sun all day long, and there is little to no shade. There are some fairly solid routes on the left side of the wall. The best description of the climbing here is "the holds are all good, but they just won't stay!"

If you are visiting Austin for only a couple days, don't bother hiking to this wall. It's unsafe and scary. Better times are had at other walls.

1) Buzzard's Breath (5.9)

This route is on the far left side of the wall and follows a discontinuous crack past four bolts. There are no anchors.

2) Ladrone (5.11)

This route climbs the straight line following pitons past drilled pockets. Probably solid, but the gear is old. (4 pitons, 2 top anchors) (FA – Paul Clark)

3) Masada (5.12)

(7 bolts, 2 top anchors)(FA – Paul Clark)

4) Femme (5.13)

Denoted by the peculiar key shaped hold by the third bolt. (7 bolts, 2 top anchors) (FA – Kevin Gallagher)

5) Starfish (5.12)**

This route can be done in one pitch as the rope drag is not too bad. (9 bolts, 2 top anchors)(FA – Jeff Jackson)

6) Cell Block (5.11)

This route has 4 bolts to the chains. The rock quality is questionable. (4 bolts, 2 top anchors)(FA – Russell Rand)

7) Medicine Man (5.12)

This is the second pitch of "Cell Block". Climb "Cell Block" to the chains. Continue up to the roof and move right to meet up with "Plate Techtonics" to finish. (10 bolts, 2 top anchors)(FA – Jeff Jackson)

8) Mah Jong (5.12)

(4 bolts, 2 top anchors)(FA – Karen Rand)

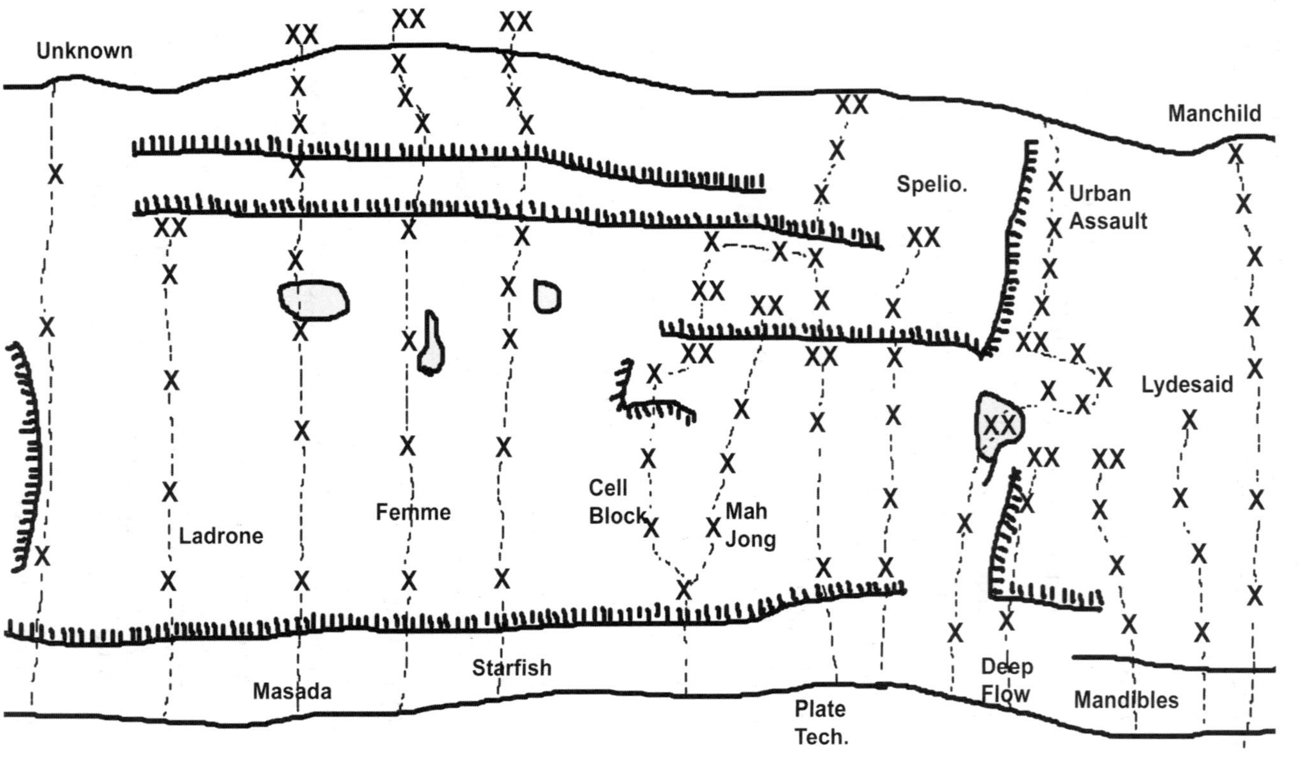

Unknown
Manchild
Spelio.
Urban Assault
Lydesaid
Ladrone
Ferme
Cell Block
Mah Jong
Masada
Starfish
Plate Tech.
Deep Flow
Mandibles

9) Plate Techtonics (5.13)

Best done in two pitches to reduce drag over the roof. (7 bolts, 2 top anchors)(FA – Jeff Jackson)

10) Spelioantics (5.12d)

11) Urban Assault (5.10b)***

Begin by climbing the dihedral on the right side of the "left oven" below the low roof, into the cave for the first belay. Climb out under the roof to an exposed move to gain the big belay ledge and onto the third pitch. Use longs slings to prevent drag. Rap from here or cruise into an exposed traverse on good hardware for a tall finish. 60 meter rope a must for rap from the top. (1st pitch 3 bolts 2 chains, 2nd pitch 3 bolts 2 chains , 3rd pitch 5 bolts 1 piton, 2 chains) (FA – James Crump)

12) Deep Flow (5.13a)

(2 bolts, 2 top anchors)(FA – Jeff Jackson)

13) Mandibles (5.12 b/c)

To the left of "Manchild" approximately 30-40 feet, ascend just right of the triangular roof, then traverse left above the roof to a thin seam to anchors. (3 bolts, 2 top anchors)(FA – Rick Watson)

14) Lydesald (A1)

(FA – Tom Lyde)

15) Manchild (5.12 R)

This is the furthest right route on the wall. Start up a dirty ramp to gain a ledge. Clip the first bolt and make a very difficult move through choss to gain a clipping stance for the second bolt. The clipping ledge has broken off, so good luck. Follow 5.9 climbing up to the saddle to clip the third bolt. Pull the roof and continue past three more bolts to the top. No anchors. (FA – Jeff Jackson)

SpyGlass Access

To find the Spyglass entrance, drive North on Mopac from Ben White (Hwy 71) for a few miles until you find the Barton Skyway exit. Turn right and drive to the dead-end and park. Hike down to the trail and head right for about three-quarters of a mile. Walk past the bike break and continue on until you find the series of walls on the right hand side.

New Wall (left to right)

The New Wall is the left most wall in the series and is often crowded. All these routes are fairly well protected and make for great leads. This is an excellent starter wall for those just getting into the harder grades. Most of the climbs here are in the 5.11 range, with a couple high quality 5.12's.

- **Random 5.8**
   This route is located about 250 yards upstream from "Flintstones" and is rarely climbed in the summer and spring months because of heavy vegetation. It is located just a few feet upstream from the turnstile (bike break). (3 bolts, 2 anchors w/ chains – hidden)

1) **Vertical Ditch (5.7 TR/trad)**
   Begin on the "Flintstones" crack and when "Flintstones" first bolt shows up on the face, stay left in the crack. Follow it for easy moves to the two bolted hangers located high and left of the "Flintstone" anchors. **Warning!** This is limestone and it breaks. Your gear and the rock may not hold! (2 top bolted hangers) (FA Ralph Showalter)

2) **Superman (5.6 TR)**
   TR from "Vertical Ditch" and about ¾ of the way, stop at the huge ledge, turn and jump to the roof a few feet away.

The rating is 5.10 if you pull the roof to the chains. (FA – Clayton Norman)

3) Meet the Flintstones (5.9)***

A high first bolt will lead one straight up to a nice stance before making an exposed move to the chains. Est.: Spring 1988. (4 bolts, 2 top anchors w/ chains) (FA – Dave Cardosa, Greg Brooks, Scott Harris)

4) Gladly, The Cross I'd Bear (5.11c)

This in one of the long traverses across the wall which is best done on a non-busy day. From the second bolt on "Flintstones" traverse right to "Mandingo" staying below the roofs of "Cloud Nine" and "Hysteria".

5) Mr. Slate (5.11a)**

Start in the dihedral right of "Flintstones". Make the crux move over the roof and finish "Flintstones". Est.: Spring 1988. (4 bolts on Slate, 2 bolts on Flintstones, 2 top anchors w/ chains) (FA – Greg Brooks, Dave Cardosa, Scott Harris)

6) Yabba Dabba Do (5.11b)**

Start as with "Schoolboys Indirect" and climb to the second bolt of "Indirect". Pull the bulge without using the crack on "Schoolboys". Finish on "Schoolboys" or "Flintstones". Est.: Spring 1988. (4 bolts via Schoolboys, 4 bolts via Flintstones, 2 top anchors w/ chains) (FA – Greg Brooks, Dave Cardosa, Scott Harris)

7) Schoolboys Indirect (5.9)***

Start just as with "Slate" in the obvious dihedral. Clip the bolt and traverse right under the roof. Make the reach over to the huge flake and go straight up. Long runners will help with rope drag on the traverse. (5 bolts, 2 top anchors w/ chains) (FA – Greg Brooks, Robert Middleton)

John Rodriquez on "Schoolboy Indirect" Photo: Mario Cantu

8) Chain Gang (5.9)

Use the start to "Schoolboy Indirect". From the flake, move right to clip the anchors on "Hysteria". Continue right to the chains of "Mandingo". This route is best done when the wall is not busy, as having your rope across that many climbs can make others a bit irritated.

9) Schoolboy Fantasies (5.11)**

Start under the flake and make the tough sequence straight up to connect with the flake. Finish as with "Schoolboys Indirect". The hard part is getting to the flake, then it eases

AustinRock
ErockOnline.com

off drastically. Est.: Spring 1988. (4 bolts, 2 top anchors w/ chains) (FA – Greg Brooks, Robert Middleton)

10) Cloud Nine (5.11d)*

Start under "Hysteria" and instead of moving right to the chicken head after clipping the second bolt, move left. Go straight up until the very end when you should traverse right to clip the anchors of "Hysteria". The crux is between bolts 2 and 3. (4 bolts, 2 top anchors w/ chains) (FA – Adam Hurst)

11) Hysteria (5.11b)***

A super classic, super pumpy climb right in the middle of the wall. The first crux is clipping the second bolt, and the second crux is having the gas to pull the roof at the top. Est.: Spring 1988. (4 bolts, 2 top anchors w/ chains) (FA – Adam Hurst, Scott Harris, Dave Cardosa, Hank Caylor)

12) Lots of People (5.11a)*

From the third bolt of "Hysteria", move right to the third bolt of "Mandingo" and finish. (5 bolts, 2 top anchors w/ chains) (FA – Rick Watson, Tony Faucett)

13) Eraser Head (5.12a TR)*

Climb the straight line from the overhang to the third bolt of "Hysteria". Set top ropes on "Hysteria" and use the third bolt as a directional. Est.: Spring 1988. (FA – Scott Harris, David Cardosa, Hank Caylor)

(Pictured on the next page: Austin (top) and Matt (bottom) working Eraser Head)

AustinRock
ErockOnline.com

14) Mandingo (5.11d)**

Just left of "Buddha" is this line. Height and flexibility are two attributes it's nice to have when pulling the crux of this route. Brut strength helps too. There is a bit of a run out between the second and third bolts. Est.: Spring 1988. (4 bolts, 2 top anchors w/ chains) (FA – Scott Harris, Dave Cardosa, Hank Caylor)

a. Dingohead (5.12b)**

This is a variation that combines "Mandingo" and "Eraser Head". Stick clip the second bolt on "Mandingo". Start on the "Eraser Head" roof, and move into the "Mandingo" crux at the second bolt. Finish "Mandingo". (3 bolts, 2 top anchors)

15) Hut Rabbit (5.11b)

Start "Mandingo" but instead of moving straight up after the second bolt, traverse right on the "Walk the Dog" ledge. Move up and back left to the third bolt of "Mandingo" and finish.

16) Girly Man (5.11b R)

From "Mandingo's" second bolt, move left over to "Hysteria" and move up to the roof, then back right to the third bolt of "Mandingo". Don't clip any bolts on "Hysteria". Potential for ground fall on the traverse. Watch for rope drag.

17) Rest and Relaxation (5.11b)

Climb "Mandingo" to the first bolt. Move left to "Hysteria's" third bolt. Continue left to the third bolt of "Cloud Nine". Move right to the anchors for "Hysteria". Climb to the bolt above then traverse right to the anchors on "Mandingo". Rope drag can be a problem if leading.

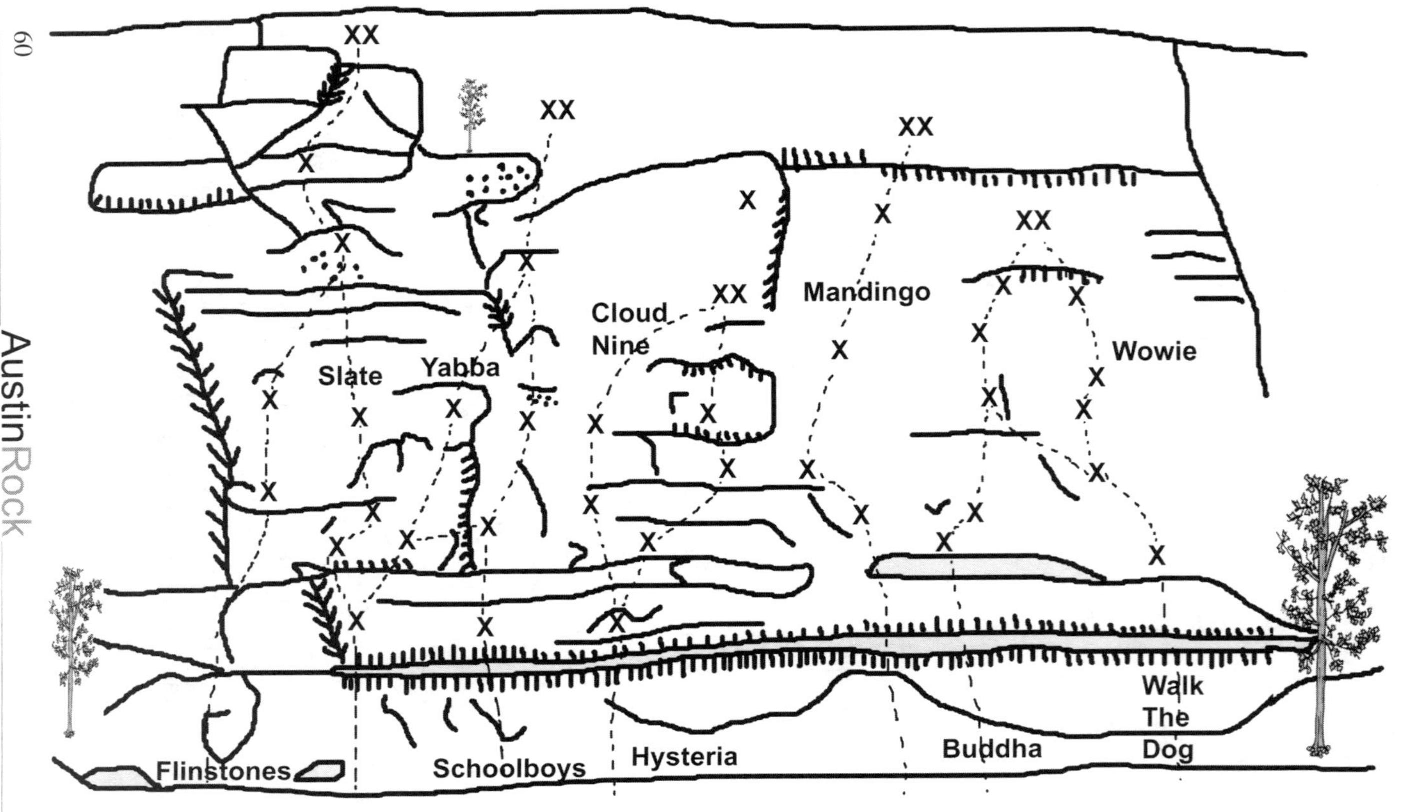

AustinRock
ErockOnline.com

18) Buddha (5.12a)***

Start in the cave and make the thin sequence to the shelf. Finish straight up on "Walk the Dog". The crux is over early, but the rest of the route will give you a pump. The top can be confusing. Some parties choose to not clip the piton above the last bolt, others prefer to use it. Est.: Spring 1988. (4 bolts, 1 piton, 2 top anchors w/ chains)(FA – Jeff Jackson)

19) Walk the Dog (5.11b)***

Start on the right side of the cave in the small dihedral. Make a smooth step to a good hold by the first clip. Move left along the small rib to make the reach over to the shelf on "Buddha" and another bolt. Finish "Buddha". Est.: Spring 1988. (4 bolts, 1 piton, 2 top anchors w/ chains) (FA – Hank Caylor, Dave Cardosa, Scott Harris)

20) Rabbit Hut (5.11c)

From the third bolt on "Walk the Dog", traverse left, staying below the roof of "Hysteria". Continue to "Slate" and finish on "Flintstones". This is a long traverse that is best to do when the wall is not busy. (FA – Rick Watson)

21) Wowie Zowie (5.11a)

From the second bolt of "Walk the Dog", go straight up instead of traversing left as with "Walk the Dog". Climb to the anchors for "Walk the Dog". (3 bolts, 1 piton, 2 top anchors w/ chains) (FA – Hank Caylor)

The Terrace (left to right)

The Terrace is the small section of non-overhanging limestone between the New and Great Walls. There are two moderate routes here, great for the new climber, and for use as warm ups for the harder stuff on either side.

1) Crystal New Persuasion (5.10c)**

This is the left most climb on the Terrace. The crux is at the top where a strong move is needed to pull the small bulge. An easier variation is found to the left of the bulge. Est.: Spring 1988. (3 bolts, 2 top anchors)(FA – Calvin Hiser, Hank Caylor)

2) Cactus Patch (5.10a)**

This route is technically easier, but the start is pretty tough and confusing. Pull the dicey first move then cruise to the anchors above. (3 bolts, 2 top anchors)(FA – Tony Faucett)

Great Wall (left to right)

The Great Wall holds the largest concentration of hard routes in the Greenbelt. Nearly all routes are 5.11 and harder.

1) Evan's Gate (5.11 TR) ***

Start standing on the boulder between "Cactus Patch" and "Heaven's Gate". Use the potato chip right toe to make a long reach to a small crimp. Top rope off "Cactus Patch". (FA – Evan Jackson)

2) Heaven Can Wait (5.11a)

Est.: Spring 1988 (FA – Scott Harris, Dave Cardosa)

3) Heaven's Gate (5.11b)**

Start on the far left of the wall and pull past three bolts to get under the roof and a no hands rest. Traverse right under the roof past three more bolts and then reach out over the shelf. Continue moving right through the hard bit and finish on the right side of the bulge above. Finish on "Hug Thy Mother" chains. This route is difficult to clean unless someone follows the route. Est.: Spring 1988. (9 bolts, 2 top anchors) (FA – David Cardosa, Scott Harris)

4) Heaven's Hug (5.11)

Climb through the first three bolts of "Heaven's Gate" and instead of traversing right, immediately pull the roof, clip the old pin to the right, and finish on "Hug Thy Mother". (FA – Tommy Blackwell)

5) Hug Thy Mother (5.12c)***

This route is great for those who are limber. Climb to the first roof and make an awkward, powerful move over the top. Get a no hands rest above then make the sequence to the next crux at the top. The last bolt is a bit run out and is a strong move to make the clip out right. (8 bolts, 2 top anchors) (FA – Tony Faucett)

6) Wind Chimes (A2)

This route probably hasn't been climbed since its FA. You can still see one old piton with blue webbing on it in the crack under the roof. (FA – David Cardosa)

7) Disneyland (5.13)**

This is the hardest line at the Greenbelt, and gets very few ascents. (5 bolts, 2 top anchors) (FA – Alex Catlin)

8) Iron Man (5.12a)***

Start below the dihedral under the roof. Make a reachy move to the top of the dihedral under the roof and get a rest. To reduce rope drag, don't clip the piton at the rest, instead clip the bolt over the lip. The climbing gets substantially easier to the top. Est.: Spring 1988. (5 bolts, 1 piton, 2 top anchors with links) (FA – Scott Harris, Dave Cardosa, Greg Brooks)

Hire a qualified guide to this area at Rock-About.com

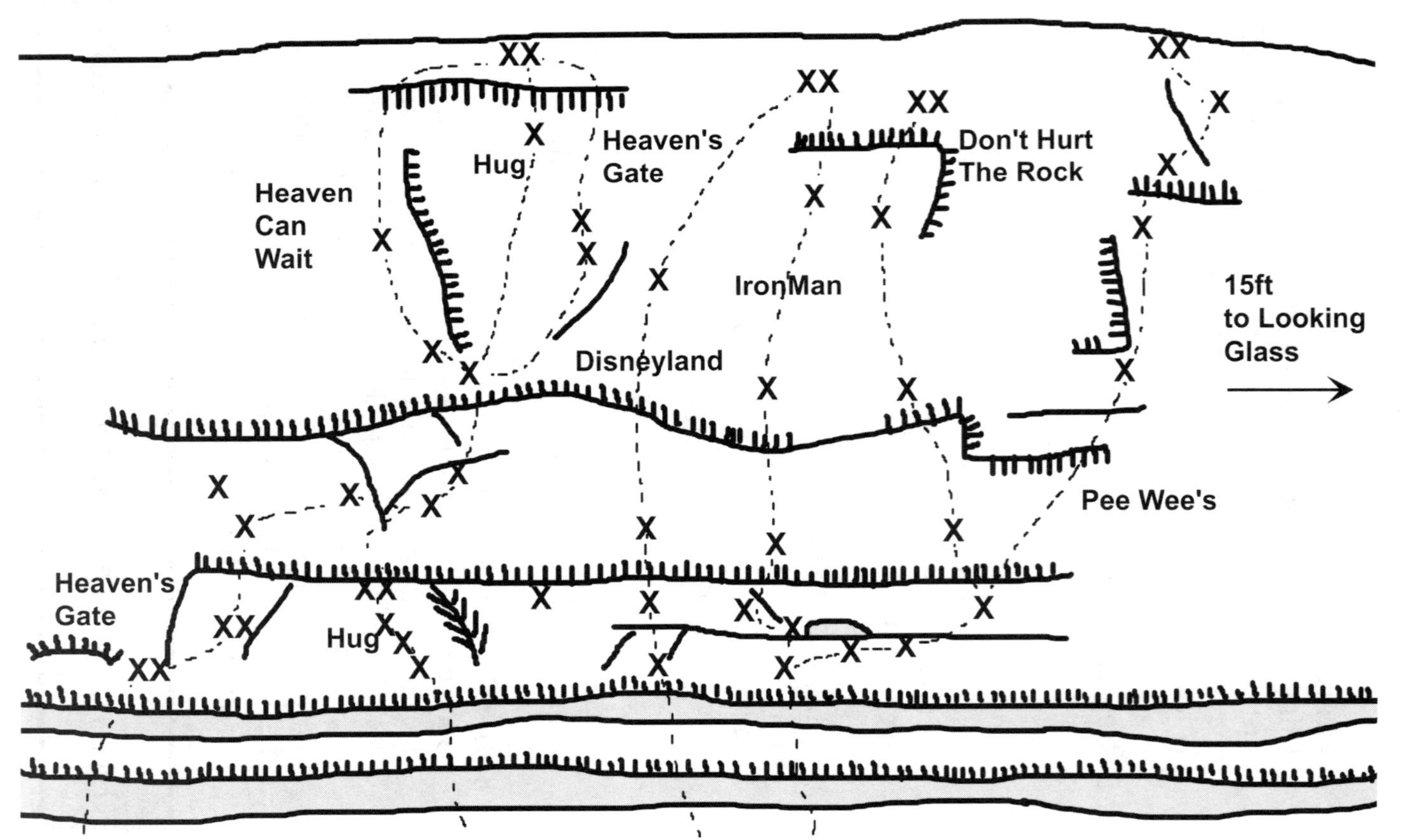

Heaven Can Wait
Hug
Heaven's Gate
Don't Hurt The Rock
IronMan
Disneyland
15ft to Looking Glass
Pee Wee's
Heaven's Gate
Hug

9) Peewees Big Adventure (5.11c)***

Clip the first bolt of "Iron Man" and move right following several bolts up to the roof around the corner. There is an excellent ledge after the 4th bolt to rest on. The 5th bolt is a bit high. The anchors are now on the face, where the 8th bolt used to be. (7 bolts, 2 top anchors w/ chains) (FA – David Cardosa)

10) Don't Hurt The Rock (5.11)

This line was put up in violation (see bolting policies). It is sparsely bolted and not really climbed. (FA – Unknown)

11) Adam's Way (5.12 TR)

This route has one piton under the first roof and then follows "Peewees" to the top. The first moves under the lower roof are now missing a hold, and is likely much harder than the rating suggests. Top rope off "Peewees Big Adventure" using long slings to reduce rope drag. Est.: Spring 1988. (FA – Adam Hurst)

12) Through the Looking Glass (5.11a)***

This is a great warm-up route for the Great Wall area. The tree stump is usually considered on route. Climb to a rest stance left of the bulge. Move out onto exposed territory, clip the bolt, and make the lunge to a good hold below the roof. A harder variation is to not use the rest stance before the bulge. Est.: Spring 1988. (5 bolts, 2 top anchors with chains) (FA – Dave Cardosa, Scott Harris, Greg Brooks)

13) Tunnel Vision (5.12a)***

This is the ultra classic line providing a fine ride. Start just right of "Looking Glass" off the baseball hold. Move up and right to the ledge. Lunge for the beak and pull through the ledge to the crux move at the top. Pull the bulge at the top and mount the crest to reach the anchors. Superb!! Est.: Spring 1988. (4 bolts, 2 top anchors w/ chains) (FA – Jeff Jackson)

Valeria Camnasio on "Through the Looking Glass" Photo by Tim Stich

AustinRock
ErockOnline.com

14) Girlie Vision (5.11c)**

Start on "Tunnel Vision" and at the second bolt move slightly left instead of making the dyno to the beak. Finish "Tunnel Vision". (FA – Jack Lawrence)

15) Tunnel Vision Indirect (5.11c)***

Climb "Tunnel Vision" up to the last bolt. Instead of moving left to the left hand crimp, move right and stand up on the ledge. Reach up to decent holds then move back to the left on slightly easier terrain to the "Tunnel Vision" anchors. (FA – Dave Cardosa, Scott Harris)

16) Channel 99 (5.12a) **

This is a contrived line that moves left from "Tunnel Vision's" fourth bolt. Don't go all the way back to "Through the Looking Glass", but stay left of the crimper used on "Tunnel Vision". (FA – Jeff Olson)

17) Eye of the Storm (5.11c)

From the second bolt of "Tunnel Vision", move right to finish "Power Monkey". (FA – David Cardosa)

18) Power Monkey (5.12d)**

This very powerful route has pulled more than its fair share of tendons. Pull the extremely tweaky starting moves to get to the second bolt, then ride the monkey to the anchors straight up. Est.: Spring 1988. (4 bolts, 2 top anchors)(FA - David Cardosa, Scott Harris)

19) Shock the Monkey (5.12d)

At the second bolt of "Power Monkey" move left to the third bolt of "Tunnel Vision" and finish. (FA – David Cardosa)

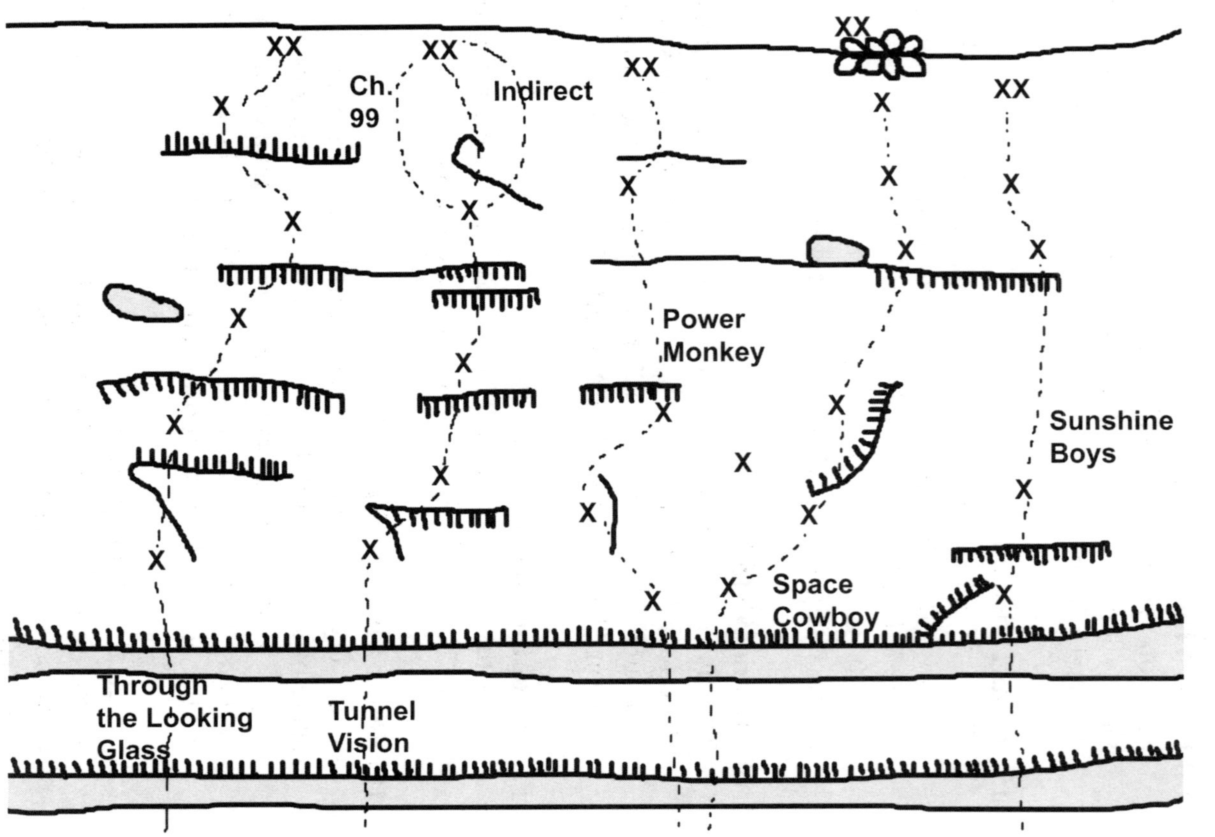

AustinRock
ErockOnline.com

20) Space Cowboy (5.12b)***

Originally called **"Zebop"**. To the right of "Power Monkey" this route takes a strong move off two small holds to a ledge. The dyno is tough since you get poor feet. If you blow it clipping the second bolt you could deck. Est.: Spring 1988. (5 bolts, 2 top anchors w/ chains) (FA – Hank Caylor, Dave Cardosa, Scott Harris)

21) Space Monkey 99 (5.12d)**

This is another bastard creation stemming from being too strong for ones own good and creating new routes to keep oneself entertained. Start under the "Space Cowboy" roof and traverse into "Power Monkey". Pull the "Power Monkey" crux and follow "Shock the Monkey" over to "Tunnel Vision". Finish on "Channel 99" to the anchors of "Tunnel Vision". (FA – Jordan DeLong)

Geritol Wall

1) Sunshine Boys (5.11c)**

Pull through the roof using a small nipple hold under the roof and a high foot on the ledge. A great knee bar is found once over the ledge. Another crux move awaits at the top. Stick clip the first bolt for safety. (FA – Scott Harris)

2) Rock and Roll High School (5.11b)***

Start 10 feet to the left of "Cedar Fever" off the dirt covered ledge. Follow the first three bolts straight up to gain the ledge. Move slightly left to the next bolt. The crux is between the 4th and 5th bolts. (6 bolts, 2 top anchors) (FA – Scott Harris)

3) Cedar Fever (5.10d)***

This is the far right route on this wall. An excellent route with fun moves. (5 bolts, 2 anchors)(FA – Scott Harris)

Valeria Camnasio on "Cedar Fever". Photo by Tim Stich

AustinRock
ErockOnline.com

Random Walls

The Random Walls refers to the small section of vertical limestone to the right of the New/Great area that is passed enroute to the New and Great Walls. These climbs have a somewhat obvious trail leading to them from the main passage. The trail is about 5 feet long. Heh!

1) Gunsmoke (5.10)

From "Cedar Fever", walk to the right on a faint trail for about 10 yards to find a small notch in the trees that leads up to the base of this route. The first part of the route is very chossy. The crux is just after the second bolt, but the rest of the route is no harder than 5.9. If a route could get negative stars, this would be it! (4 bolts, 2 top anchors)

2) Hank's (5.10)

This route is about 100 yards downstream from "Gunsmoke". Slab moves to the first bolt, 5.8 moves to the second bolt hidden on top of the ledge. Crux comes in clipping and moving over the fourth bolt. (4 bolts, 2 top anchors) (FA – Hank Caylor)

3) Tiddlywinks (5.9 X)

This route is about 25 feet tall and just a little ways down from "Hank's". No bolts, no anchors. (FA – Jeff Jackson)

The Enclave

The Enclave is usually passed over by everyone eager to get down to New and Great Wall. From the Spyglass entrance, turn right on the trail just as you would to get to the New/Great Walls. About half way there you will see what appears to be a gully that splits off the main trail going right. Hike down that gully for about one minute. You will see an obvious arête on a beautiful boulder right in the middle of the open area.

1) Arrow Head Arête (V3) ***

As you approach the nest of boulders in the Enclave, this arête will likely be the first thing that catches your eye. A beautiful layback arête that beckons to be climbed. Once you unlock the beta and make a successful ascent, the fun continues by eliminating holds under the arête.

Sean O'Grady on "Arrow Head Arête". Photo: Tommy Blackwell

2) Arrow Head Arête (low feet) (V5)***

Climb "Arrow Head" without using any heel hooks. This makes it a tad more difficult.

AustinRock
ErockOnline.com

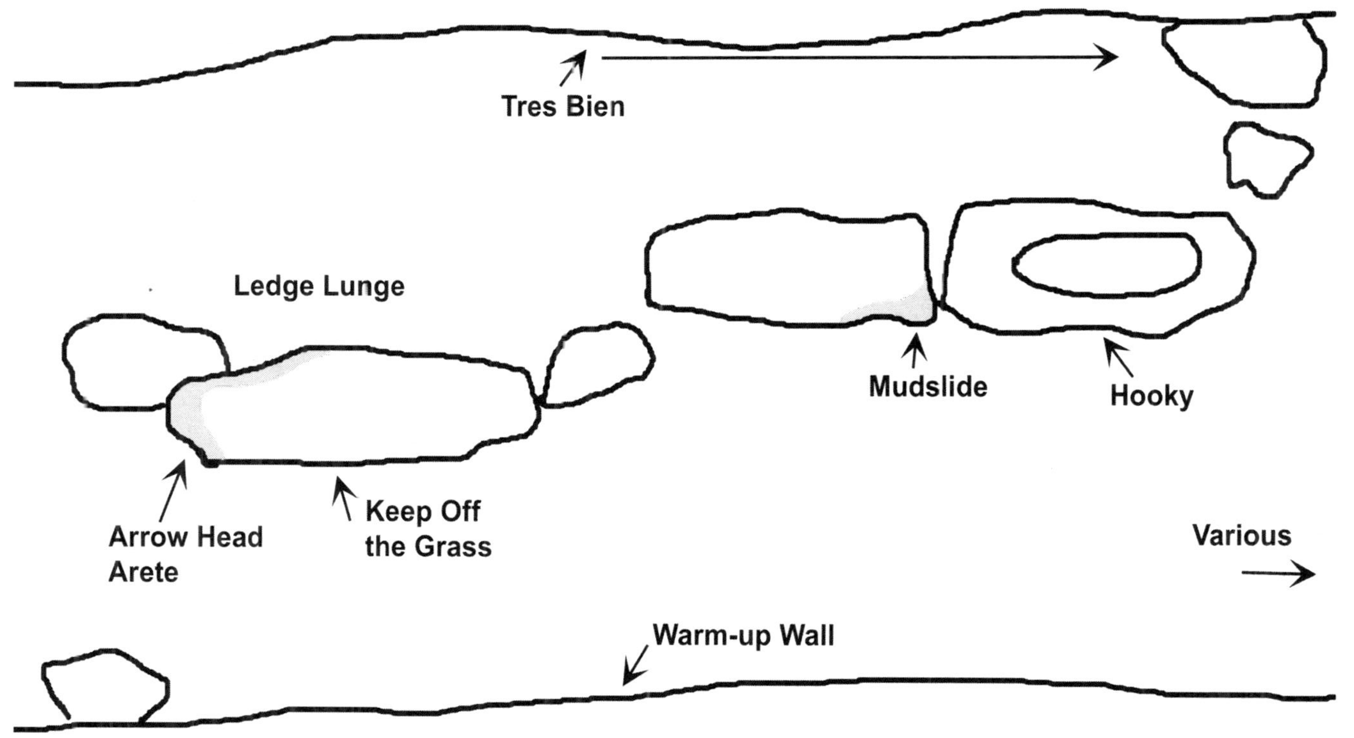

Tres Bien
Ledge Lunge
Mudslide
Hooky
Arrow Head
Arete
Keep Off
the Grass
Various
Warm-up Wall

3) Ledge Lunge (V4)**

Just left of the arête is a serious back breaking venture that starts down in the notch. Make a couple long dynos onto some sharp holds until you can top out.

4) Keep off the Grass (V0-)*

This is a fun little slab problem to the right of the arête. The challenge is trying to not touch any of the lichen on the up climb and down climb. Fun for laughs!

Sean O'Grady playing "Hooky". Photo: Tommy Blackwell

5) Mudslide (V?)

This problem is actually under the boulder located behind the arête boulder. Crawl into the little cave-like entrance a few feet. Climb out of the cave and top out on the boulder. This problem is usually muddy.

6) Hooky (V3+)**

Denoted by the two dish holds to start, this problem encourages nifty body dynamics to maintain stability. Topping out is somewhat difficult because the rock quality turns from solid to crap up high.

7) Tres Bien (V4+)***

On the wall behind the boulders holding the above problems is this fun ride. At one time the word "EXIST" was written in chalk on the far left to denote the start of the route. Traverse to the right until you can step off.

Campbell's Hole (left to right)

To get to Campbell's Hole, park at the Spyglass entrance just as with the New/Great Wall areas. Hike down to the trail and turn left. Look for a tall wall on the other side of the creek. This area is tough to get to when the water level is high. This area is never really used as a climbing destination, but more of a swimming and hang out destination by non-climbers. The routes are old, and not maintained. Bush-whacking is needed to get to the base of the routes. They are listed here mainly to preserve the information that they exist, but there is no beta for them.

1) Holy Diver (5.12)

(FA – Hank Caylor)

2) Gravity's Angel (5.11)

(FA – Calvin Hiser)

Zilker Access

To get to Zilker Park from South Austin, take Mopac (Loop 1) north to the Barton Skyway exit. Stay on the access road and you will end up on Barton Springs. Turn right into the Barton Springs parking lot (second right turn on Barton Springs) and park at the south end by the theater. Follow the trail from the south end of the parking lot.

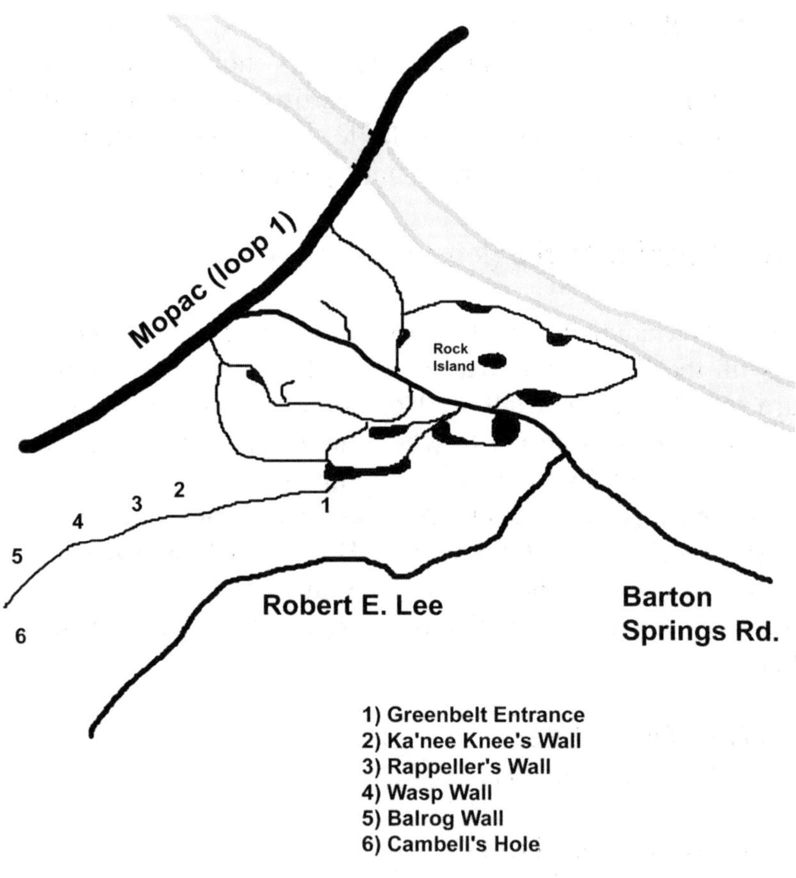

AustinRock
ErockOnline.com

Ka'nee Knee's Wall

From the Zilker entrance to the greenbelt, hike in about ¾ of a mile or so until you find a small, obvious rock outcrop on the right side of the trail. There are three large boulders that now lie close to the trail as a result of rock fall above the wall. Because of this, some of the problems listed here may be no longer climbable. On the right side of the bluff is a roof with a horizontal crack under it. The following boulder problems are found here.

1) Ka'nee Knee's Bane (V3)
Start on the right side of the horizontal crack and make the face sequence left to mount the roof. Top it out over the second lip for a complete send.

2) O Risk a Knee (V3)
Start on "Ka'nee Knees Bane" and traverse left along the horizontal crack. Where the tree is closest to the wall is where you begin to top out.

3) Orbit (V3)
Traverse "O Risk a Knee" and instead of topping out, high traverse right back to the beginning of "O Risk a Knee" via "Ka'nee Knee's Bane".

4) Tunnel Vision (V3)
Start in the cave left of the tree and top out.

Rappeller's Wall

A quarter mile past Ka'nees Knees the trail and the rock come close together. There looks like there was once a gate that went across the trail before the wall as there are still three telephone sized posts, one with cable still attached. There is potential for routes with bolts here, although not very exciting. In the middle

of the wall, just left of the overhang, is a low angle ramp that leads to what may be exciting moves at the top. There are no top rope anchors, and taking the time to set up a route is hardly worth the effort. In fact, if you are in town for a couple days, this wall is not worth the hike in.

1) The Sink (V2)
Find the small cave at ground level, to the left of the wall. Start inside and climb out, anywhere.

2) The Plumber (V3)
Exit "The Sink" to the right on thin side clings

Wasp Wall (right to left)

Two to three hundred yards past Rappeller's Wall is Wasp Wall, which is slightly hidden by trees. Locate the semi-obvious path to reach the base of the wall. This wall is supposed to be on private property now, as the home owner at the top of the wall had his property line moved from the top of the cliff to the bottom several years ago. He hated climbers so much that he chopped the anchors off the top while a climber was mid-route. Afterwards, he began throwing trash and trees off the top to discourage anyone from climbing on his wall ever again. The area is now lost, and not worth the trouble.

1) Classic (5.4)
This is a somewhat obvious dihedral that is pretty much unreachable because of the huge beaver-like damn structure at its base.

2) Holtzendorf Direct (5.7)
(FA - Harold Holtzendorf)

3) Mosquito (5.9)
(FA – James Crump)

4) Wasp (5.8)
(FA – James Crump)

5) Rush (5.10)
(FA – James Crump)

6) Atomic Rush (5.10c)
(FA – Bill and Paul Horton)

Balrog Wall

This is the next big wall with houses on top. There could be potential for reviving this wall as well, but because of lack of interest, trash, and commercial grade poison ivy at the bottom, no one really bothers going. The routes are listed here because during the golden age, this wall was more accessible.

1) Zipper Lounge (5.10a)
This route climbs the obvious dihedral that can be seen from the trail. (FA – Garth McGee)

2) Rocket Pocket (5.10c)
(FA – James Crump)

3) Balrog (5.11a)
(FA – James Crump)

4) Head Trip (5.11)
(FA – Dave Head)

5) Tit Scratch (5.11)
(FA – James Crump)

6) McClure/Sanders Traverse (V3)
Traverse the sloping lower band

Frank's Meat Market

Frank's Meat Market is the obvious bluff on the right and left side of the 360 bridge as you head north on Hwy 360 from South Austin. The "Bridge" referred to is the large, arching bridge that goes over Lake Austin. Park in the gravel cut-out on the North side of the bridge, but not in front of the "no parking" signs. Walk up the ramp to the top where you will find a nice trail leading into the woods. About 100 yards in is a somewhat obvious down climb, which is also a bit scary since the ground tends to crumble under your feet. Another option is to anchor to a tree and rap down. **Warning: wear long pants as the area is rarely visited and thorn bushes and poison ivy own the land.**

There are a couple bolted routes here without anchors, as well as a crack that can be seen from the road. The quality of the bolts is questionable as is the rock. This area gets so little attention that bolt maintenance has likely never been done.

On the other side of the bridge (the west side) is a couple of routes of equal or better value. To get there, hike up the ramp on that side and hike down the obvious trail about a quarter mile or so. Using the flag poles across the lake as a point of reference, anchor a rope from a tree and rap in. There are about 4 routes, some with old bolts, and some without bolts at all. The grades range from 5.9 to 5.12.

Franks Wall East (left to right)

1) Left Arête (5.7)

2) Franks Crack (5.9)

This crack is easily seen from the road and is usually the cause of climbers venturing over to the market in the first place. The crack goes at 5.9 all the way to the bolt below the roof. If you climb the roof, the rating is about 5.11. (FA – Dave Hannah)

3) Franks Meat Market (5.11)
(FA – James Crump; FFA – Jeff Jackson)

4) Franks Direct (5.12)
(FA – Jeff Jackson)

Franks Wall West (left to right)

1) Hammerhead (5.12d)
This route is directly under the overhang on the left end of the climbing portion of the wall. There are 4 bolted on gym holds through the roof section. (4 bolts, 2 top anchors w/ chains) (FA – Hank Caylor; 1994)

2) I Do (5.11)
(FA – Kirk Holliday, Brian Wann; 1994)

3) Unknown (5.11)
This route has one bolted on gym hold. (FA – Charle Chapman; 1993)

4) Woofin Hooters (5.11)
This is the far right route with a low first bolt and a manky third bolt. (FA – Hank Caylor, Randy Harris; 1986)

Road Cut (North West Side)

1) Road Pizza (5.9)
This bolted route is on the road cut on the North side of the 360 bridge. The route is old and the bolts are bad. Climbing this route might also land you a ticket. (FA – Hank Caylor; 1987)

Pace Bend Park

John Gonzales at Pace Bend. Photo: www.merrickales.com

Pace Bend Park

Pace Bend is the number one summer climbing destination in Austin. Pace Bend is approximately 30 miles west of Austin on Lake Travis. From the intersection of RR 620 and Hwy. 71, take Hwy. 71 west 11 miles to RR 2322 (Pace Bend Park Road). Turn right on RR 2322 and travel 4.6 miles to the park entrance.

Park Fees:

- Day Permit -- $8.00 (per vehicle)

- Pedestrian / Bicyclist -- $3.00

- Primitive Camping -- $15.00 (per vehicle)

- Improved Camping -- $20.00 (per vehicle)

There are three main climbing areas inside of the park. All roads into the coves from the main road are dirt roads, and are passable by regular passenger vehicles. There are generally no "parking" areas, as most folks just pull their cars out of the way and bail out.

When climbing at Pace Bend, it's a good idea to bring rafts, floaties, and other such things so that you are not treading water all day, as the energy expense will dampen your fun. A water proof camera is a good idea as well.

The water level varies at different times of the year, and during times of low water, you may be in for a 30 foot jump into water of unknown depth. Be very aware of the water depth before jumping in. Pace Bend is fun, but can be extremely hazardous if you do not think about the environment you are climbing in.

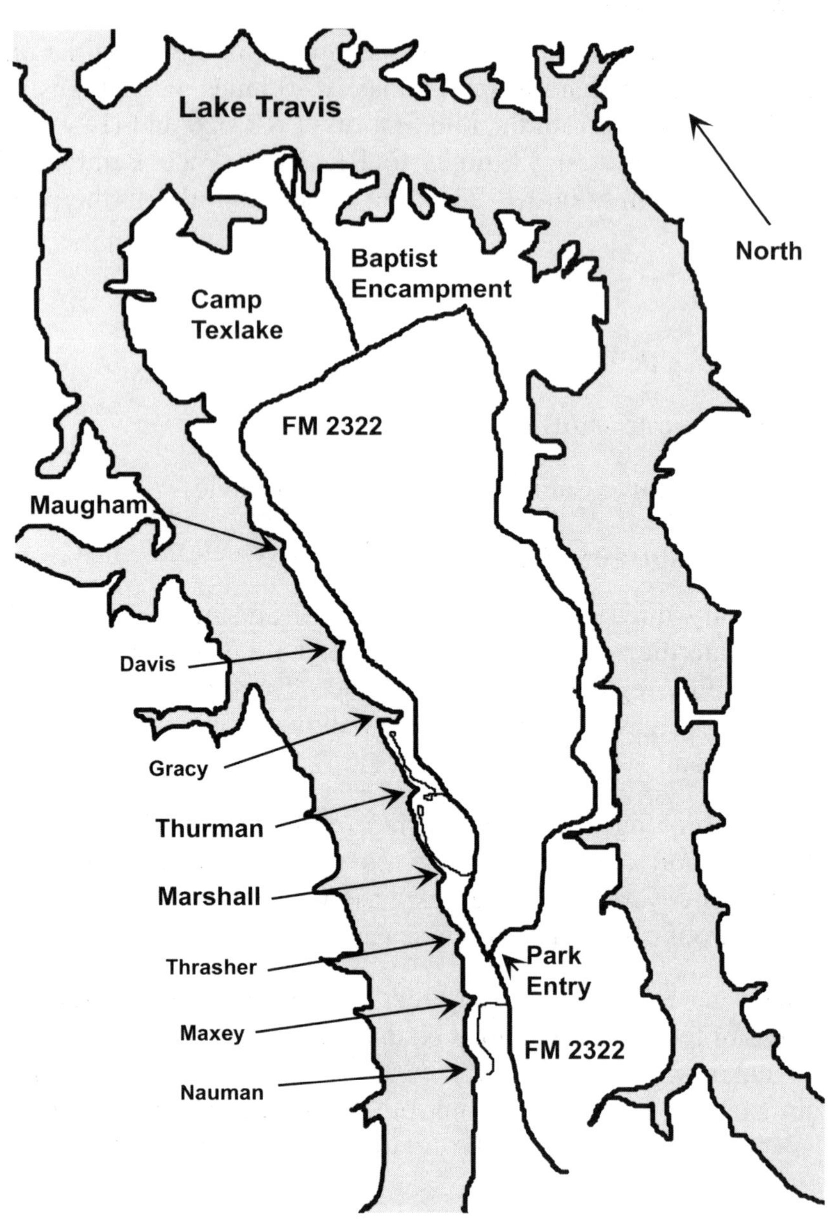

AustinRock
ErockOnline.com

Marshall Cove

Marshall Cove is the first area in Pace Bend that has any notable climbing. There are several routes here that you can use a rope for, which may not be a bad idea during times of low water. Be watchful of the quality of the bolts, however, since they spend most of their life underwater. Some of the bolt counts here may be wrong since they may have rusted off. Most folks just climb and fall into the water. The route names are listed here more for historical reference.

1) Something (5.11)
   (4 bolts, anchors?)(FA – Kirk Holladay, Bill Gooch)

2) Mysterious White Hand (5.9)
   This route is 30 yards to the right of "Something".
   (3 bolts, anchors?)(FA – Kirk Holladay, Bill Gooch)

3) Baby Don't Break (5.10)
   (4 bolts, anchors?)(FA – Kirk Holladay, Bill Gooch)

4) 5.10
   (3 bolts, anchors?)(FA – Kirk Holladay, Bill Gooch)

5) 5.7
   This route is about 20 yards to the right of the 5.10. (3 bolts, anchors?)(FA – Kirk Holliday, Bill Gooch)

6) 5.7
   (3 bolts, anchors?)(FA – Kirk Holladay, Bill Gooch)

Thurman Cove

Thurman Cove is an area with a high density of juggy overhanging routs. There are bolted lines here as well, but when the water is high, there is little to no need for the rope. Bring your floaties and jump in. Climb, fall, jump, repeat.

Sean O'Grady at Thurman Cove. Photo by Bryan Thome

AustinRock
ErockOnline.com

1) Spider Baby (5.10a)
There once were 4 bolts on this route. Possibly they are still there, but with the changing water levels, they may be useless. (FA – Kirk Holladay, Alvino Pon)

2) Black Sunshine (5.11)
(5 bolts, anchors?) (FA – Kirk Holladay, Alvino Pon)

3) Dude From Dallas (5.8)
(2 bolts, anchors?)

4) Head Boat (5.11b)
(FA – Dave Head)

5) Voyage of the Boat People (5.12)
(FA – James Crump)

6) Bay of Pigs (5.12)
(FA – James Crump)

7) Plight of the Haitian Refugees (5.10)
(FA – James Crump)

8) Traverse From Plight (5.10)
(FA – James Crump)

Maugham Cove

Maugham has many nice short problems with little to no bolted lines. It is the last cove with any notable climbing, as everything past this area is almost absent of rocks. The climbing here is slightly less overhanging than that found at Thurman. It's a good place to go when the water level is lower. Enjoy!

Bull Creek Park

Bull Creek is perhaps one of the most overused areas in town, not necessarily by climbers per se, but in general. The unusual amount of graffiti on the back of the front side boulders make one want to cringe. Many of the holds on the front side boulders are super polished, and the amount of chipped routes in such a small area is amazing.

That being said, Bull Creek is a nice little gem tucked away in North Austin with a quaint bouldering scene, and a relatively untouched route database (partially due to the choss factor). Climbing skills are tested daily, causing the use of normal smearing technique to leave you scratching you head in bewilderment. The added height to the bouldering creates a nice head game as well.

Getting There:

To get to Bull Creek Park from South Austin, take Capital of Texas Hwy (Hwy 360) North just past the bridge to 2222. Exit and turn right (east) on 2222 (Bull Creek Rd). Get in the left lane to immediately turn left on Lakewood Dr. Continue on Lakewood for about a mile to the parking area before passing over the low water crossing. The boulders will be facing the water directly in front of you. A pea gravel landing has been added to the front side because of its use as a bouldering area over the years. The wall is shaded pretty well and usually stays wet for a few days after a rain.

Boulders - Front side (Left to Right)

All problems on these main boulders have a common down climb – the low angled ramp/ledge on the right side of the right boulder. The descriptions start on the left most vertical boulder and work right, over to the easier angled slab on the right.

1) Ruffles Have Redges (V3)
Climb the left arête next to the stairs to the top. (FA – James Crump)

2) Bull Huecos (V4)
Start on "Ruffles" and traverse the top of the entire boulder. Descend "Romex", stem over to "Screaming Fingers" and do the high "Crump Traverse". (FA – Mike Head)

3) Viagra (V9)
Start between the two white streaks of chipped rock following enhanced holds to top out just left of the lichen stripe. (FA – Hank Caylor)

4) Xanax (V5)
Start on two high crimps (the right crimp is reinforced with glue) and pull up to a left hand pocket. Find two more pockets above and an interesting finish. (FA – Hank Caylor)

5) Prescription Child (V6)
Start on "Xanax" and follow crimps and pockets to finish on "Viagra". (FA – Hank Caylor)

6) Tiny Dancer (V7)
Start in a small dish and pull past many little monos to gain a nice dish 4 feet from the top. (FA – Hank Caylor)

7) Walter Weed Shuffle (V5)***
This is the route to the right of "Tiny Dancer". Start in the obvious shallow pocket with the left hand and the higher right crimp. Climb to the 3 pocket cluster. Unlock the tough top out sequence just left of the arête. (FA – James Crump)

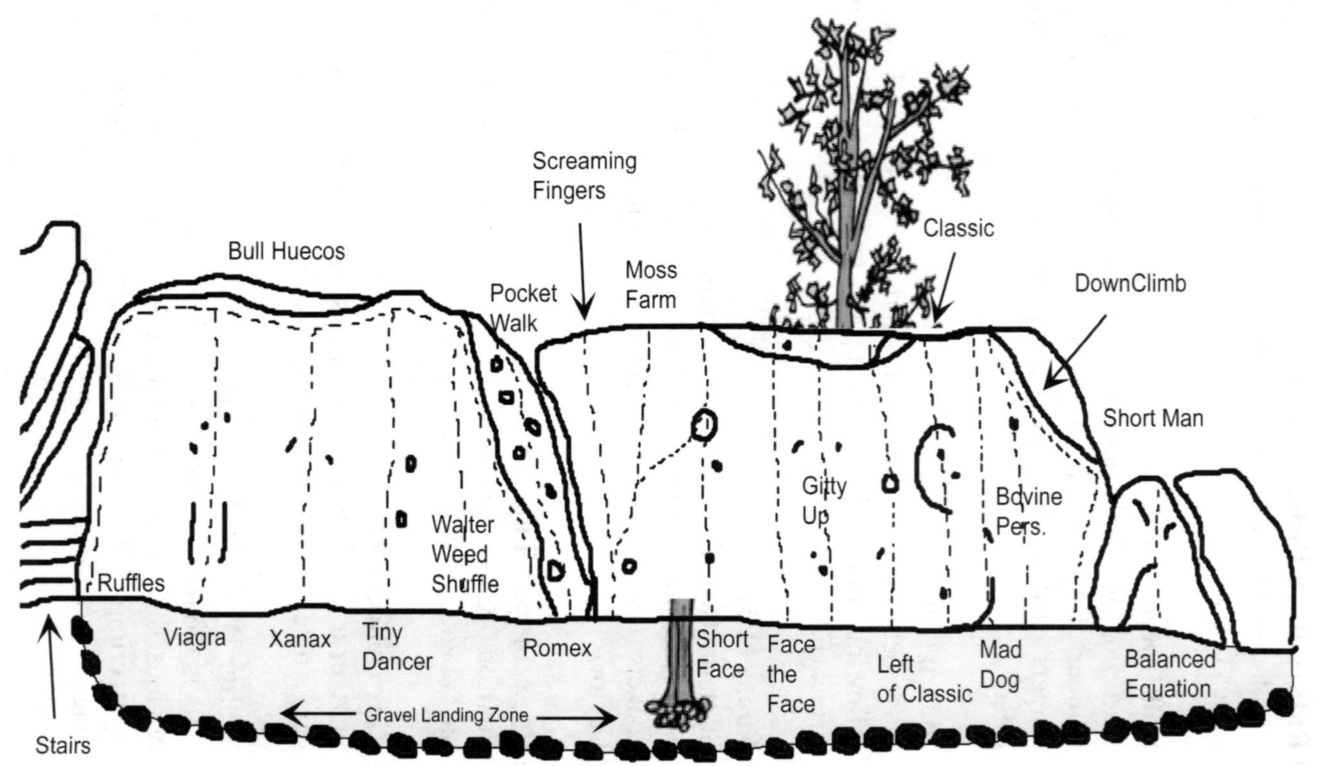

Screaming Fingers
Classic
DownClimb
Bull Huecos
Moss Farm
Pocket Walk
Short Man
Gitty Up
Bovine Pers.
Walter Weed Shuffle
Ruffles
Viagra
Xanax
Tiny Dancer
Romex
Short Face
Face the Face
Left of Classic
Mad Dog
Balanced Equation
Gravel Landing Zone
Stairs

8) Romex Reality Shuffle (V1)

Layback the right most arête keeping your feet low on the face. Finish without traversing all the way over to the left. (FA – James Crump)

9) Pocket Walk (V0)

Climb the obvious pocketed face just right of the arête. (FA – James Crump)

10) Chimney Shorts (V0-)

Use chimney techniques to climb up between the two main boulders. (FA – James Crump)

11) Screaming Fingers (V0)**

Found on the far left side of the right boulder. There is an obvious series of pockets that seem to get smaller the higher you go. A great warm-up. (FA – James Crump)

12) Moss Farm (V3)

Use the starting holds of "Screaming Fingers" and move up and right just as the moss begins, using small pockets and monos. Finish straight up just right of the moss and just left of the big, obvious hueco. Don't chicken out and dive into the hueco. Resist! (FA – James Crump)

13) Dazzling Desperation (V2)

Start just as with "Moss Farm" but move into the hueco above and finish straight up. There is also a double jump variation, jumping to the big hueco, then to the top. (FA – James Crump)

14) Short Face (V2)

Start directly under the big hueco using small holds including monos and polished crimpers to gain the pocket. Pull to the top from there. Don't use the obvious three finger pocket from "Moss Farm" and "Dazzling Desperation". (FA – James Crump)

15) Face the Face (V2+)

Start directly under the drilled mono using one of the small, obvious pockets for your right hand. Work your way up to a nice crimper. Move through the sloping dish to the top. Top out just left of the little tree. (FA – Bill Gooch or James Crump)

16) Gitty Up (V2+)

Use one of the two pockets on "Face the Face" for your left hand, and a nice side pull for your right. Stand up and reach a deep pocket and then move into the sucker dish. Top out just right of the small tree. (FA – Bill Gooch)

17) Left of Classic (V1)

Stay on the left side of the obvious rock scar on the boulder. Start in a hand sized hueco and move straight up.

18) Classic (V0)

Climb through the middle of the obvious rock scar on the wall using small, deep pockets and good feet to reach the top. (FA – James Crump in 1972)

19) Mad Dog and Beans (V1+)

Use a pocket and a left angling, right facing crimp to start. Climb up the right side of the rock scar using high steps and deep pockets to the top. (FA – James Crump)

20) Bovine Perspiration (V2+)

Start off a small rounded crimp on the right side of the wall and climb through small pockets and monos to the top. Make the long reach from the dish to the top. (FA – James Crump)

21) Short Man (V0)

The furthest right side of the boulder, climb the short face to the lower ledge of the boulder. There is really only one or two moves, and it's over.

22) Short Hands (V2+)

Climb "Short Man" and traverse below the ledge over to "Bovine". Use pockets below the ledge only.

23) Bill Creek Traverse (V4)

Traverse low staying below or even with the obvious rock scar all the way across. The going starts to get tough around the drilled mono. (FA – Bill Gooch)

24) Crump Traverse (V4)

This is a high traverse across the wall. Start on "Screaming Fingers", climb half way up "Pocket Face" and begin moving right using pockets of various sizes to gain the ledge on the right side of the wall. (FA - James Crump)

25) Little Wimpy (V1)

This is the little crack found in the boulder just right of the main boulder. Start sitting and finger jam to the top out. Fun, but short.

26) Balanced Equation (V0)

This is a great no hand problem on the same boulder as "Little Wimpy", only it's on the front slabby side. Put your hands behind your back and balance your way to the top using decent incut feet. Crazy man!!!

Backside (Left to Right)

1) West End (V0)

On the far left end of the backside is a short slab with a seam running down it. Climb the seam using whatever you can. This problem will leave you wondering where the pockets are. (FA – Bill Gooch)

2) The Point (V1+)

Just to the right of "West End" is this arête. Grab the point on the arête and smear up on bad feet. Mantle from the point to the top. (FA – Bill Gooch)

3) Freaking Feet (V1+) *

Start with hands on the obvious rail to the right of the arête. Paste the left foot on and bring the right foot into the upper hueco. Bring a high left foot and make the balancey move to the top to exit.

4) Lip Lunge (V2-) *

To the right of "Freaking Feet" using both lower huecos for the feet. Grab the rail with the left hand, put the right foot in the bottom pocket. Bounce up to a two finger, half pad divot, bring the left foot up to the upper hueco, and lunge for the lip.

5) Hole in Wall (V4) ***

Start with a high right hand on an obvious crimp. Use the left hand for balance and get your feet on small nubbins. Dyno for the lip. Possibly manufactured, but it's hard to tell. Super fun!

6) Pocket Sleuth (V5)

Start right of the tree on the moss and paint covered portion of the wall. "T-Bone Stallone" is painted over this route. Use small pockets and awkward feet. Move up to the broken seem then to the tough top out.

7) Pocket Locket (V5)

There are a couple obvious huecos here. Grab the manufactured pocket, and do you best to reach the hueco above. A challenging top out is made no easier by the chipped holds.

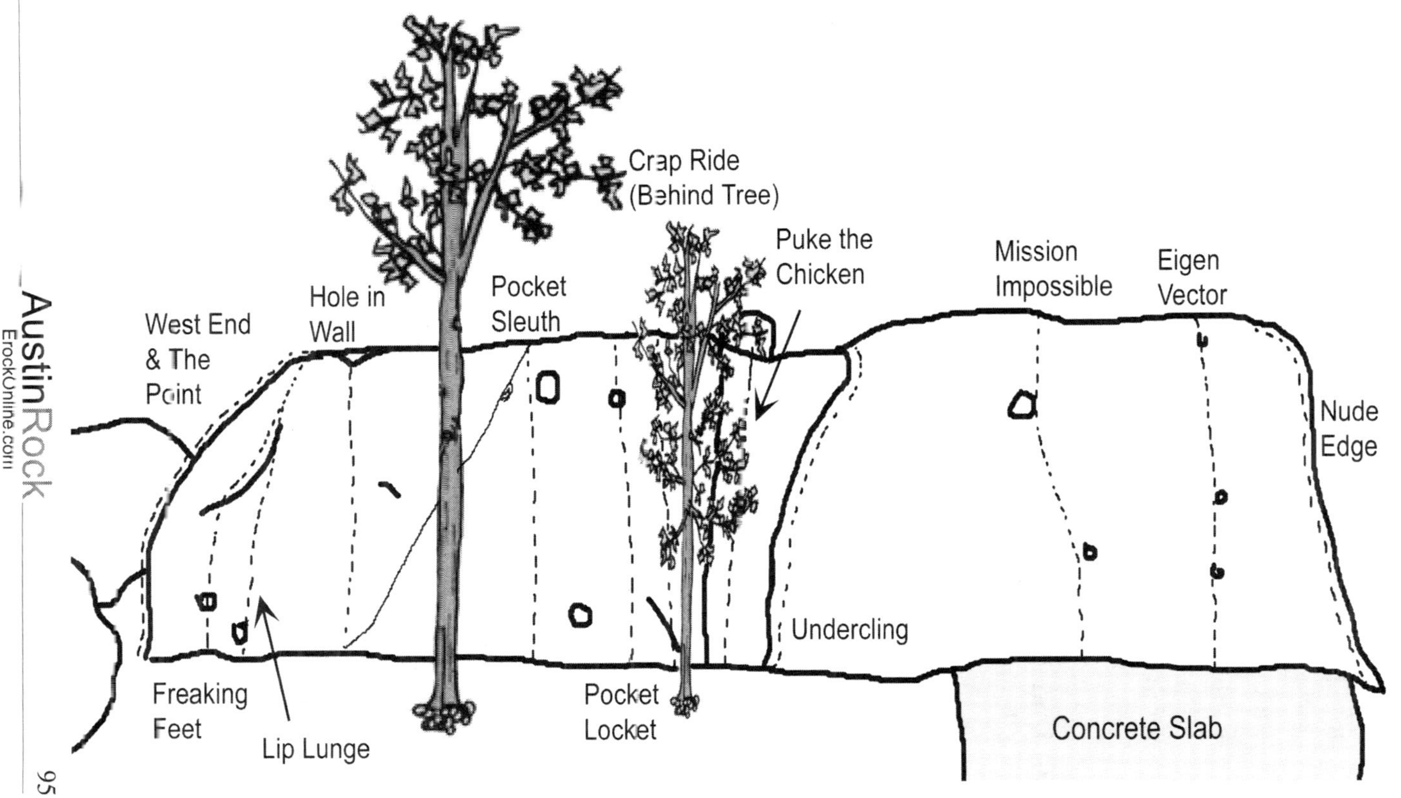

West End & The Point
Hole in Wall
Crap Ride (Behind Tree)
Pocket Sleuth
Puke the Chicken
Mission Impossible
Eigen Vector
Nude Edge
Undercling
Freaking Feet
Lip Lunge
Pocket Locket
Concrete Slab

8) Crap Ride (V5)

Start left of the tree and make several thin moves to the top. Likely chipped.

9) Puke the Chicken (V1)

Climb the choss between the two boulders using face holds left of the under cling to the diving board boulder above. Grab it, cut your feet, and bounce. The rock will dance for you. Top out when bored. (FA – James Crump)

10) Undercling (V2)**

Climb the obvious layback arête using small feet to the top of the boulder. (FA – James Crump)

11) Mission Impossible (V5)

Start from the drilled mono to the left of the "Pink Floyd" graffiti. Dyno to the hueco (or use some other creative method) and mantle over the top. (FA – James Crump)

12) Eigen Vector (V7)

Use the obvious drilled mono above "Floyd" (once used to hold shower stall in place) and make a desperate pull to a small, invisible crimp and one last real pocket to gain the ledge to top out. (FA – James Crump)

13) The Nude Edge (V2)

Climb the obvious arête to the top. More challenging if you start sitting. Even more challenging if you traverse the top all the way across. (FA – James Crump)

Big Chief Boulder (Left to Right)

This is the lone boulder to the left of the stairs on the other side of the concrete slab. There are several easy little problems here, most of which are sit starts.

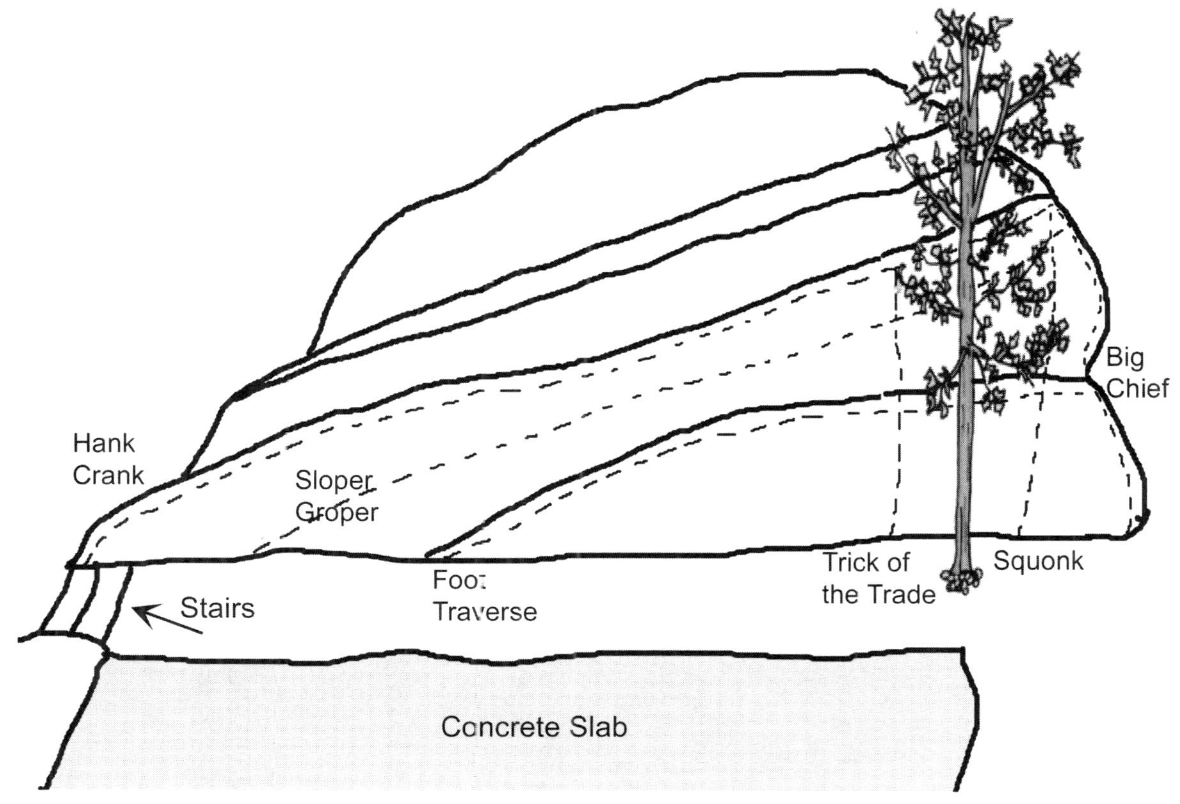

Hank
Crank
Sloper
Groper
Stairs
Foot
Traverse
Trick of
the Trade
Squonk
Big
Chief
Concrete Slab

1) Hank Crank (V1)
Start sitting on the stairs and traverse right along the large ledge system. (FA – Hank Caylor)

2) Sloper Groper (V1)
Traverse right on holds below the ledge for "Hank Crank".

3) Foot Traverse (V1)
Start sitting and traverse right on the lowest possible ledge system. Finish on "Big Chief".

4) Trick of The Trade (V1)
Start sitting to the left of the tree and finish on "Hank Crank". Avoid the large hueco to start.

5) Squonk (V2)
Start sitting to the right of the tree and finish straight up avoiding the arête. (FA – James Crump and Bill Gooch)

6) Big Chief (V0)
Climb the arête on the right side. For a tougher variation, sit start the problem.

The Library Wall (Right to Left)

To get to the here, locate the faint trail on the North side of the low water crossing. Walk through the corridor of huge overhanging limestone to find the Library Wall just as the overhang begins to end. Climbing here is a mixed blessing because the wall is technically on private property, but the property owner allows us to climb here. However, the rock and bolt quality is so questionable that climbing here is the closest thing to insanity as you can come without being committed. The topo included here is not complete, since to get more accurate beta would involve climbing these routes. I'm not insane!

1) Altered States (5.12)
This route has some fantastic drilled pockets, complete with drainage holes. (FA – Greg Brooks)

2) Project
This route may never be completed. Instead of project, it maybe should be called "Abandoned".

3) Gulliver's Travels (5.12d)
(FA – Jeff Jackson)

4) Atlas Shrugged (5.12)
(FA – Jeff Jackson)

5) Surrender (5.12)
(FA – Jack Mileski)

6) Finnegan's Wake (5.13d)
This route starts on the right side of the graffiti.

7) Kubla Kahn (5.13)
Start at the bolt line found in the middle of the graffiti. (FA – Jeff Jackson)

8) Metaphysics (5.12c)
(FA – Jeff Jackson)

9) Lord of the Flies (5.12)
(FA – Russell Rand)

10) Blatant (5.12a)
This route meets "Lord of the Flies" and finishes on that route. (FA – Dave Head; FFA – Mike Head, Scott Harris, Larry Spears)

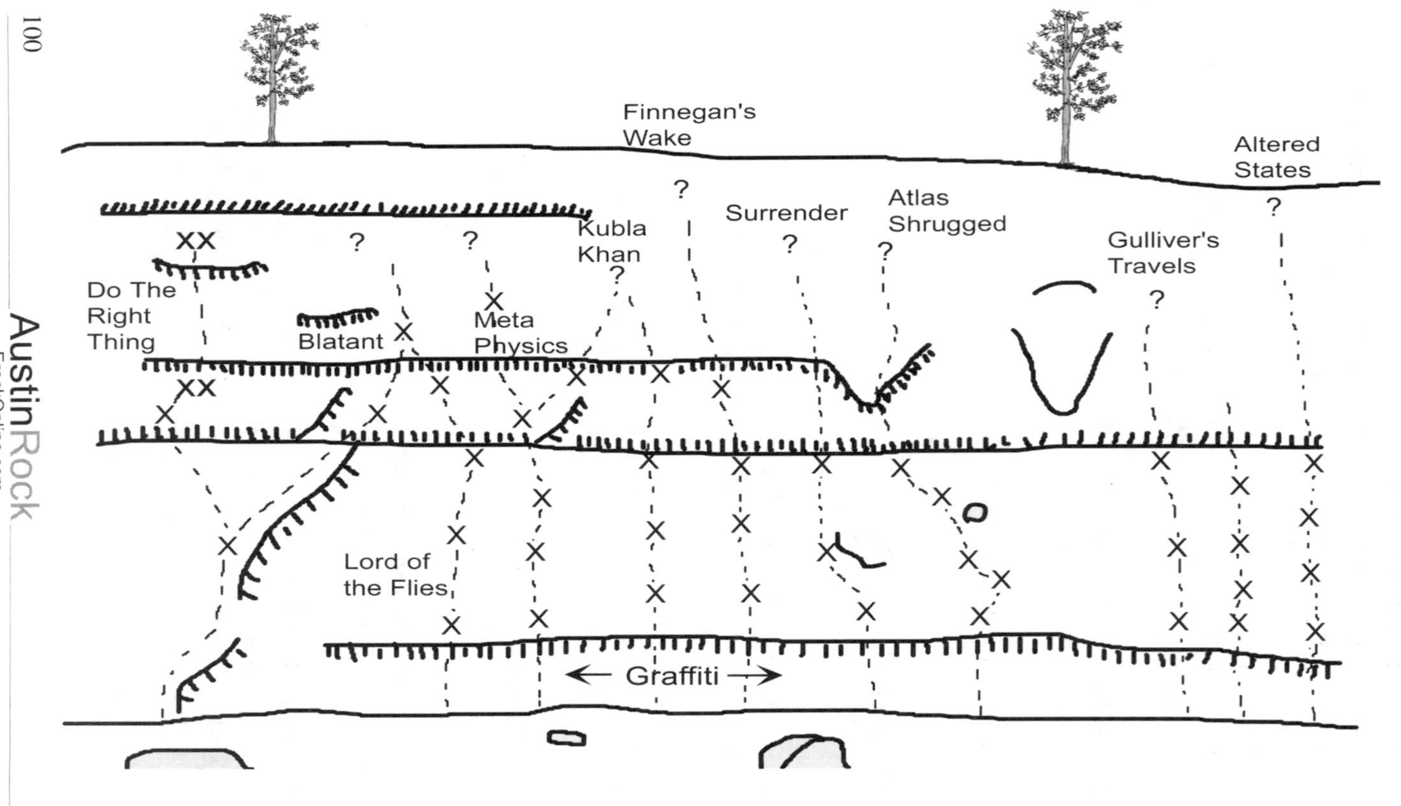

Finnegan's
Wake
Altered
States
?
Surrender
Atlas
Shrugged
?
Kubla
Khan
?
?
?
Gulliver's
Travels
?
Do The
Right
Thing
Blatant
Meta
Physics
Lord of
the Flies
← Graffiti →

11) Do the Right Thing (5.12a)
This route can be done in two pitches to reduce rope drag.(FA – Jeff Jackson)

Bonzo Wall (right to left)

The Bonzo Wall is the next wall with a smattering of bolts. The topos shows that bolts exist, but the quality of the bolts is questionable, just as the rock is. Very little if any useful beta is included. Climbing here is dangerous and will most likely result in injury. Have Fun!

1) Minerva (5.11c)
This route is found several feet to the right of "Chemical Warfare". (FA – Elaine Catlin)

2) Chemical Warfare (5.11a)
(FA – Greg Brooks)

3) Beans and Rice (5.12a)
(FA – Jeff Jackson)

4) Head Thing (project)
The bolts are supposed to angle to the right, if they are even still there…

5) Bonzo's Revenge (5.13)
(FA – Hank Caylor)

6) Bedtime for Bonzo (5.11)
Start off the left side of the leaning boulder and climb straight up to the old bolt. From there head right and finish on "Bonzo's Revenge". (FA – James Crump)

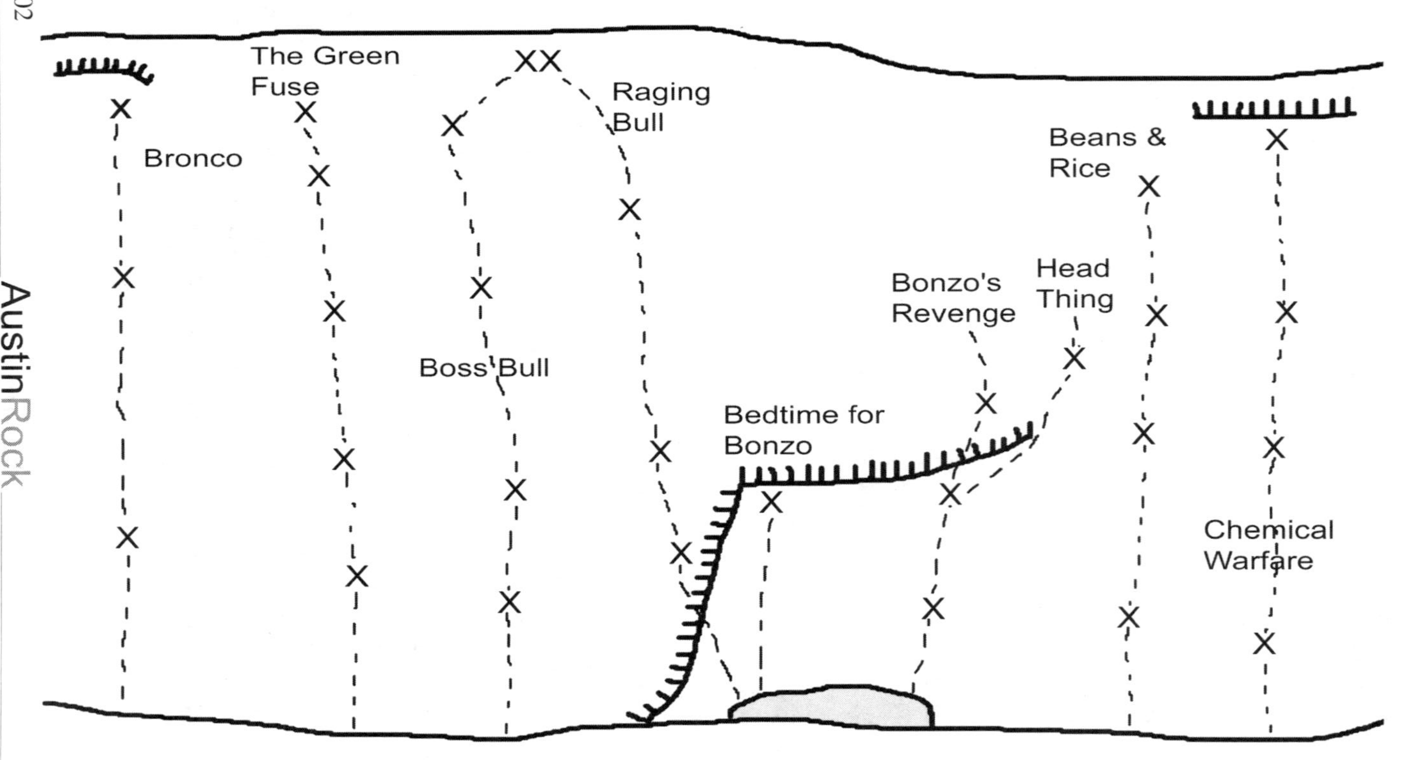

AustinRock
ErockOnline.com

7) Italian Route (A2)
(FA – James Crump)

8) Raging Bull (5.12a)
This route climbs the arête to the left of "Bedtime for Bonzo". (FA – Jeff Jackson)

9) Boss Bull (5.12a)
(FA – Jeff Jackson)

10) The Green Fuse (5.12a)
(FA – Jeff Jackson)

11) Bronco (5.12 R)
(FA – Jeff Jackson)

12) Ricks Traverse

Far Wall

The Far Wall is located about 200 yards downstream from the Bonzo Wall and holds one established route.

1) Gooched (5.11)
(FA – Bill Gooch)

Reimer's Ranch

Matt Twyman on "Irreverent Youth". www.merrickales.com

Reimer's Ranch

Reimer's Ranch is located in Dripping Springs, right outside Austin. It has great access and is one of the premier limestone crags in town. There are several ways to get there. From Hwy 620, from Southwest Parkway, or from the Y in Oak Hill, go North on Hwy 71 until you come to Hamilton Pool Road (RR 3238). Turn left and go about 11.5 miles until you find a green fence on the right side that says "Reimer's Fishing and Climbing Ranch". Drive down the dirt road (go left at every fork) until you come to the house (about 3 miles). Pay the $5 entry fee and continue around the dirt road until you see the parking area with the two porta-pots. The trail to the climbs is located to the right of the nice green sign.

The routes and walls are described in order starting on the right side of the area, and then go to the left side, moving down the wall sequentially.

Reimer's Ranch is closed Monday and Tuesday and Wednesday, and they close the gates when it gets dark. Don't get stuck inside after dark. They hate that!

An Early History of Reimer's Route Development:

By Tom Suhler

All of the routes below strictly followed the Traditional Reimer's Naming Convention: Upon finishing a day of climbing and/or bolting we would adjourn to the Chuy's on Barton Springs for margaritas, beer, & Mexican food. Once our brains were well lubricated we would start the serious work of conjuring up the appropriate name for our newest route.

Dead Cats Don't Meow – Dave Cardosa, Tom Suhler. This was the 3rd climb added to this wall. In the beginning there was Reimerama & Water Ballet. This was the first route Tom bolted. Big thanks to Dave for showing me the tips and tricks of route selection, bolt placement (testing for solid rock and good clipping stances), cleaning (removing loose rock with crowbars), and gardening. During the bolting of this climb we discovered the small grave of Emma Peel which was located close to the cliff. A rock that served as a tomb stone had the following inscription "Here lies Emma Peel. She was a good cat."   It was always our intention to come back and do another route in the same area named Emma Peel. **Almost Nothing To It** – Tom Suhler, Maggy the rock dog. Named for the little crux that hits you at the top, just when you start to think there's … **Centipede** – Dave Cardosa, Tom Suhler.   Immediately after bolting and completing the first accent of this route, one of those large 10 inch centipedes came crawling out of one of the finger pockets we had been using all day. **Spider Grind** – Dave Cardosa, Tom Suhler, Duane Cardosa. While bolting this route there was a LARGE spider (it seemed to be at least 4 inches, but was probably more likely 8 inches in diameter) under one of the ledges directly above us. It just sat there all day, checking us out, while we bolted the route. **Zoe's First Step** – Tom Suhler, Rick Tamplin. Greg Brooks and I climbed together for awhile. He would belay me on climbs like Telegraph Road and then I would belay him on climbs like Rust Never Seeps. Then Greg met Suzee. Then Suzee joined us and we all went climbing together. Then Suzee started bringing her yet to be born daughter with us. Then 9 months later Zoë joined us in diapers and we all went climbing together. And finally on Father's Day 2005, Zoë ascended this route. **I Never Called You a Beast** – Tom Suhler, Rick Tamplin. Once upon a time Rick had a girl friend. And on one rainy day Rick said something that really pissed her off. Well she let fly a tirade so foul and venomous that propriety prevents the printing of it here. Several months later, after they had broken up, Rick ran into her at the store. He recounted the litany of things she used to describe him including the fact that he had "acted like a beast". After listening to his recounting of her diatribe, she contemplated his rendition of her speech and then calming replied, "well Rick, I never …" **Maggie's Farm** – Tom Suhler, Rick Tamplin. Rick is a huge Bob Dylan fan and we both loved Maggy the rock dog. **Tit for Tom** – Dave Cardosa, Tom Suhler. Tom's girl friend at the time was not particularly well endowed. In fact the stalactite used to pull the crux of this climb was reported to be approximately the same size as her… **Ant Encounters** – Tom Suhler, Maggy the rock dog. Not the best line I ever put up. And damn there were a bunch of ants.

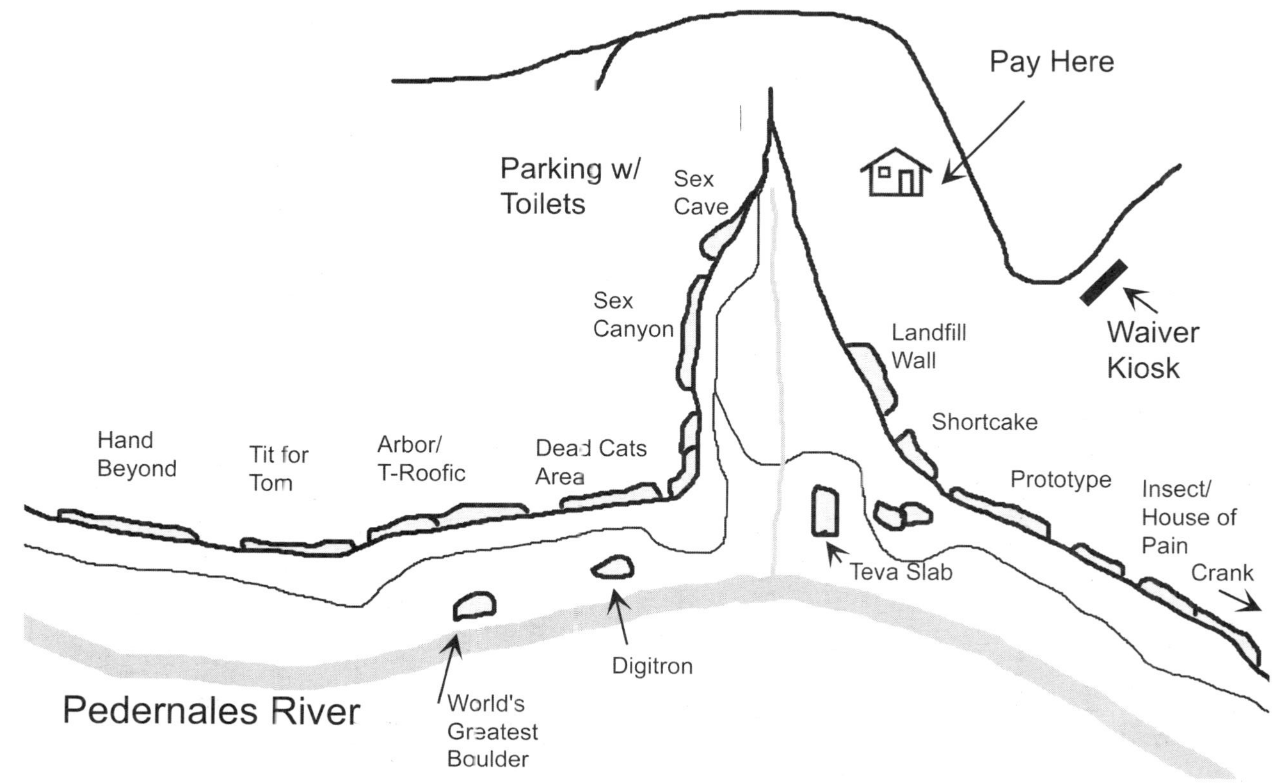

Pay Here
Parking w/ Toilets
Sex Cave
Sex Canyon
Waiver Kiosk
Landfill Wall
Shortcake
Prototype
Insect/ House of Pain
Crank
Hand Beyond
Tit for Tom
Arbor/ T-Roofic
Dead Cats Area
Teva Slab
Digitron
World's Greatest Boulder
Pedernales River

Sex Cave (right to left)

The Sex Cave is the painfully obvious cave that everyone must pass to access the rest of the climbing walls at Reimer's Ranch. Many stalactites mark this as a fantastically picturesque area.

1) Lip Service (5.12a)
The first route encountered when entering the Sex Cave. This high traverse climbs up and then moves left. (FA – Jimmy Carse)

2) Spider Grind (5.11b)**
Traverse left using holds a bit lower than "Lip Service". (FA – David Cardosa / Tom Suhler)

3) Mud Lip (5.11)
Spider Grind Direct? Climb to the third bolt of "Spider Grind" to the roof. (FA – Russell Rand)

4) Sex Grind (5.12)
Climb "Spider Grind" to the seventh bolt of "Liposuction". Finish on "Liposuction".

5) Viper (5.12 TR)
Use "Spider Grind" anchors to climb the vertical tufa right of "Body Wax". You can "lead" it by pre-clipping the third bolt of "Spider Grind" to finish on "Mud Lip".

6) Body Wax (5.12b)***
Start off the lower ledge following bolts through the roof. If you blow it while clipping any bolt you could deck. No anchors. Down climb and clean. (FA – Jeff Jackson)

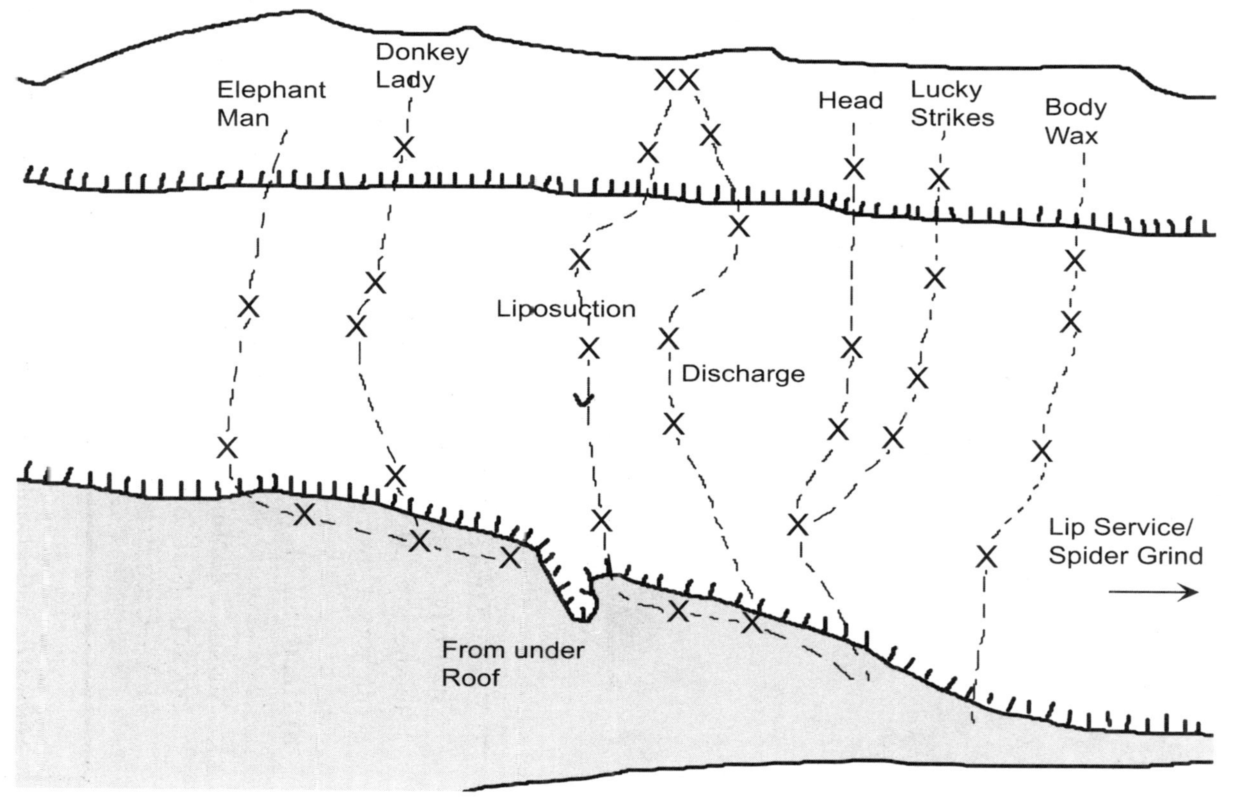

Elephant
Man
Donkey
Lady
Head
Lucky
Strikes
Body
Wax
Liposuction
Discharge
Lip Service/
Spider Grind
From under
Roof

Jordan DeLong cooling his jets on "Body Wax"

7) Lucky Strikes (5.13b)***

Start left of "Body Wax" climbing through natural pockets to the top. Move right after the first bolt. There are no anchors. Down climb and clean. (FA – Mike Klein)

8) Head (5.12d) ***

Instead of moving right after the first bolt as with "Lucky Strikes", continue straight up climbing past two drilled pockets used to pull the roof move. No anchors.(4 bolts) (FA – Greg Brooks)

Hire a qualified guide to the area at Rock-About.com

Jordan Delong on "Liposuction"

9) Liposuction (5.12a)***

Start on the ledge above the cave and traverse the roof past two bolts to gain the large, obvious stalactite. (It's recommended that you unclip the first bolt after clipping the second to reduce drag) Get a great no hands rest above the stalactite and then move into the fun stuff above. (7 bolts, 2 open angles for anchors) (FA – Greg Brooks)

10) Discharge (5.13c)

From the first bolt of "Liposuction" climb straight up to the last bolt and anchors of "Liposuction". This route used to be rated 12c, but a critical hold broke and possibly hasn't been climbed since. The rating is a guess. (FA – Rupesh Chhagan)

11) Lipo Variation (5.12)

From the no hands rest on "Liposuction" continue moving left and finish on "Elephant Man". (FA – Russell Rand)

12) Donkey Lady (5.12c)

Stupid crazy European rope management system needed to climb this route. Climb "Elephant Man" to the second bolt and head towards the face. If you use only one rope, you will have crazy rope drag. Permanent draws hung under the roof.

13) Elephant Man (5.13a)

Traverse the stalactites under roof and move towards the face. There once was a no hands rest at the lip, but has broken off, making the route a bit run out now. (FA – Duane Raleigh)

Sex Canyon

The Sex Canyon is the very next wall that you come to after you hike through the Sex Cave. Most of the routes are 5.11 and harder, with one route under 5.11.

14) Pulmonary Choss (5.11c)

The first bolt is questionable. (FA – Mike Klein)

15) High Anxiety (5.10c)

Starts right of two giant stalactites. Climb up through a slot with a small tree growing from it. Move through the tufa laden dish to reach the crux at the top. This is the easiest problem in the canyon. (FA – Mario Cantu)

16) Mistaken Identity (5.11c)

Starts left of stalagmites on the black streak to the right of "Telegraph Road". (FA – Greg Brooks)

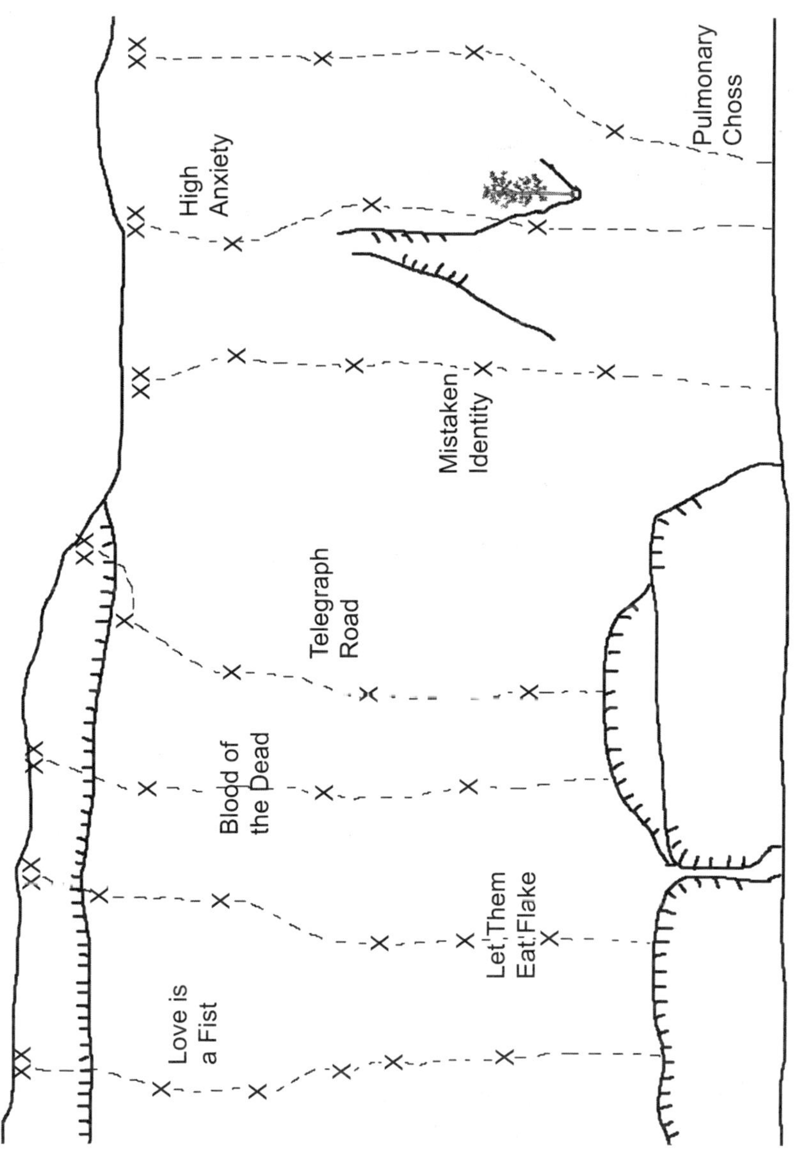

Pulmonary Choss
High Anxiety
Mistaken Identity
Telegraph Road
Blood of the Dead
Let Them Eat Flake
Love is a Fist

Michael Johnson on "Learning to Fly". merrickales.com

AustinRock
ErockOnline.com

17) Telegraph Road (5.11b/c) **

Start off a large boulder on the ledge. Climb past tufas and flakes then make the traverse right under the roof. The anchors are back a bit. (FA – Greg Brooks)

18) Blood of the Dead (5.11b)***

Start off the boulder on the left side. Start by grabbing the large flake and clip the first bolt. Follow fairly straightforward climbing up and slightly left through two more bolts. The anchors are over the bulge at the top, but the chains hang down far enough to clip without pulling the roof. (FA – Joe Sulak, who named the route "Sangre de Muertos)

19) Let Them Eat Flake (5.11d) **

Step right off a high boulder and climb straight up through the roof. (FA – Jeff Jackson)

20) Love is a Fist (5.12c)

Start off the same boulder as before, climbing straight up through drilled pockets to the top. (FA – Josh Pierce)

21) Bolus (5.12d)***

Scramble up to the start and clip the first bolt in the tufa. The second bolt is just above the obvious flake system. Make a series of hard bouldery moves to the third and fourth bolts. Jugs above the fourth bolt. There is a glued hold on this route. (FA – Mike Klein)

22) Learning to Fly (5.12b)

(FA – Jimmy Menendez)

23) Super Cruiser (5.13b)***

(FA – Tom Scales)

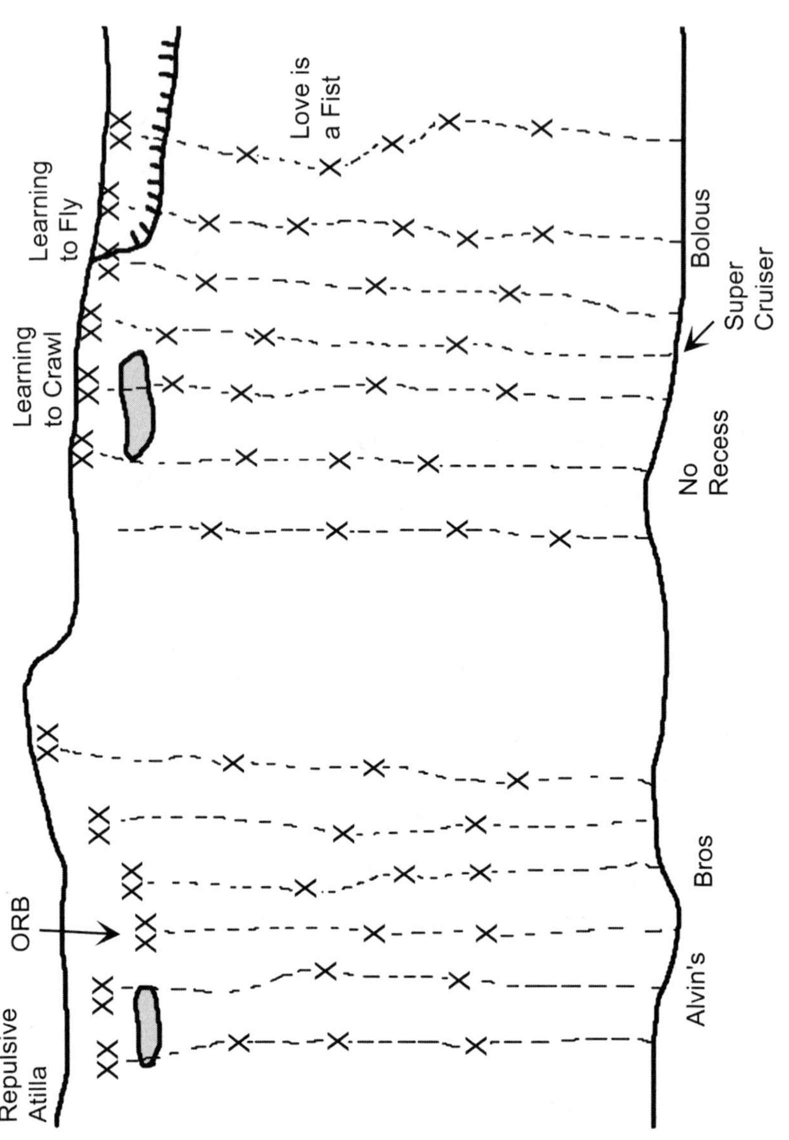

AustinRock
ErockOnline.com

John Gonzales on "Super Cruiser". www.merrickales.com

24) Learning to Crawl (5.12)

Climb through the overhang containing many stalactites. There are three manufactured pockets here, but two of them had been filled in. Use the manufactured pocket for this rating. (FA – Greg Brooks)

25) Yearning to Brawl (5.12d)

This is "Learning To Crawl" without using the manufactured pocket. (FA – Adam Strong)

26) Hyper Salivation (5.13b)

Start on "Learning to Fly". Clip the second bolt and traverse right to finish on "Bolus". (FA – Mike Klein)

27) No Recess (5.12c)

(FA – Wayne Crill)

28) unknown

29) unknown

30) unknown

31) Bros Before Hoes (5.12d)***

Climb the bulging overhang left of the dihedral. (FA – Tom Scales)

32) ORB (5.12c)

(Over-Rated Bullshit) Climb the face right of the big white streak.

33) Slick Willie (5.13a)

The Coletrane (project) was finally done and rated. (FA – Tom Scales)

34) Alvin's (5.12)

(FA – Alvino Pon)

Jordan Delong on "No Recess". www.merrickales.com

35) Repulsive Attila (5.11b)
   (FA – Alex Catlin)

36) Snuff the Rooster (5.12a)
   Climb the left side of the big white streak. (FA – Steve Hunt)

37) Friends and Lovers (5.11a)
   A Short route (20 feet) with 3 bolts twenty feet right of Zoë's Wall.

38) unknown

Zoë's Wall

Zoë's Wall is found around the corner from Sex Canyon sitting up on a little shelf. There are a few easy routes here that are worth the time to hike up to.

1) I Never Called You a Beast (5.6) **
   (2 bolts, 2 top anchors)(FA – Tom Suhler, Rick Tamplin)

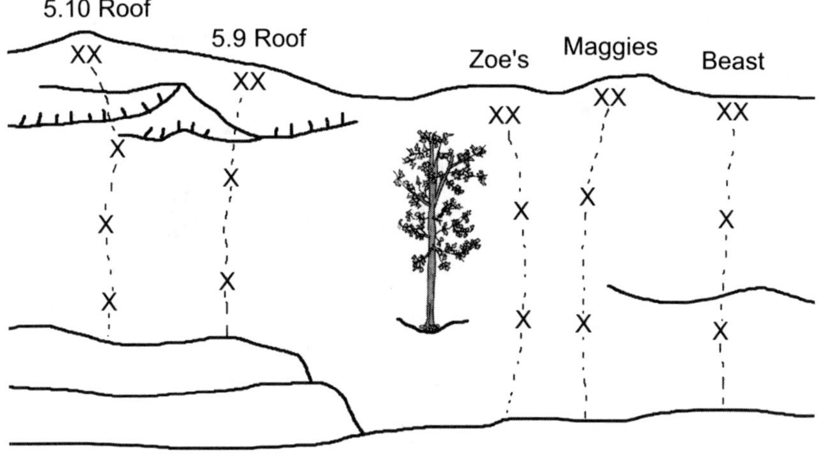

AustinRock
ErockOnline.com

2) Maggie's Farm (5.6)
   (2 bolts, 2 top anchors)(FA – Greg Brooks)

3) Zoë's First Step (5.8)
   (FA – Greg Brooks)

4) 5.9 Roof (5.9)
   30 – 40 feet left of Zoë's Wall. Follow a dihedral to a roof, and traverse right under the roof.(FA – Kevin Benz, Mario Cantu)

5) 5.10 Roof (5.10)
   Climb a dirty ledge to a bolt. The forth bolt is right of the roof. Pull roof to finish. (FA- Kevin Benz, Mario Cantu)

Serpent's Wall

This is the 25 foot wall with the roof at the base in between Zoë's Wall and the Dead Cat's Walls. Super short, but pretty fun.

1) Blank Page (5.11a)
   Start off the fallen block and move over the low roof. (FA – Kevin Benz)

2) KB-5 (5.9)
   (FA – Kevin Benz)

3) Sidewinder (5.10c) **
   (FA – Kevin Benz)

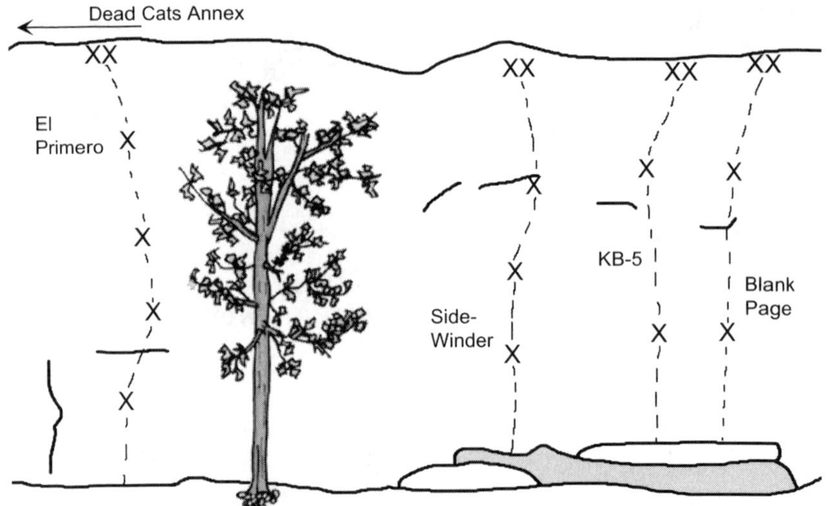

Dead Cat's Annex

If Dead Cat's Wall is packed, this is a good substitute wall as it is rarely crowded, but within talking distance to climbers on Dead Cat's Wall.

1) El Primero (5.9) *
Located about 40 feet left of "Sidewinder" in front of several small boulders. (FA – Mario Cantu)

2) Quality Ivy (5.10a)

3) Mammaz Boyz (5.9) *
This route starts in a seam. (FA – David Phillips)

4) The Sting (5.9) *
Starts to the right of a tree. There is a beehive between these two routes. Beware! (FA – Joey Phillips)

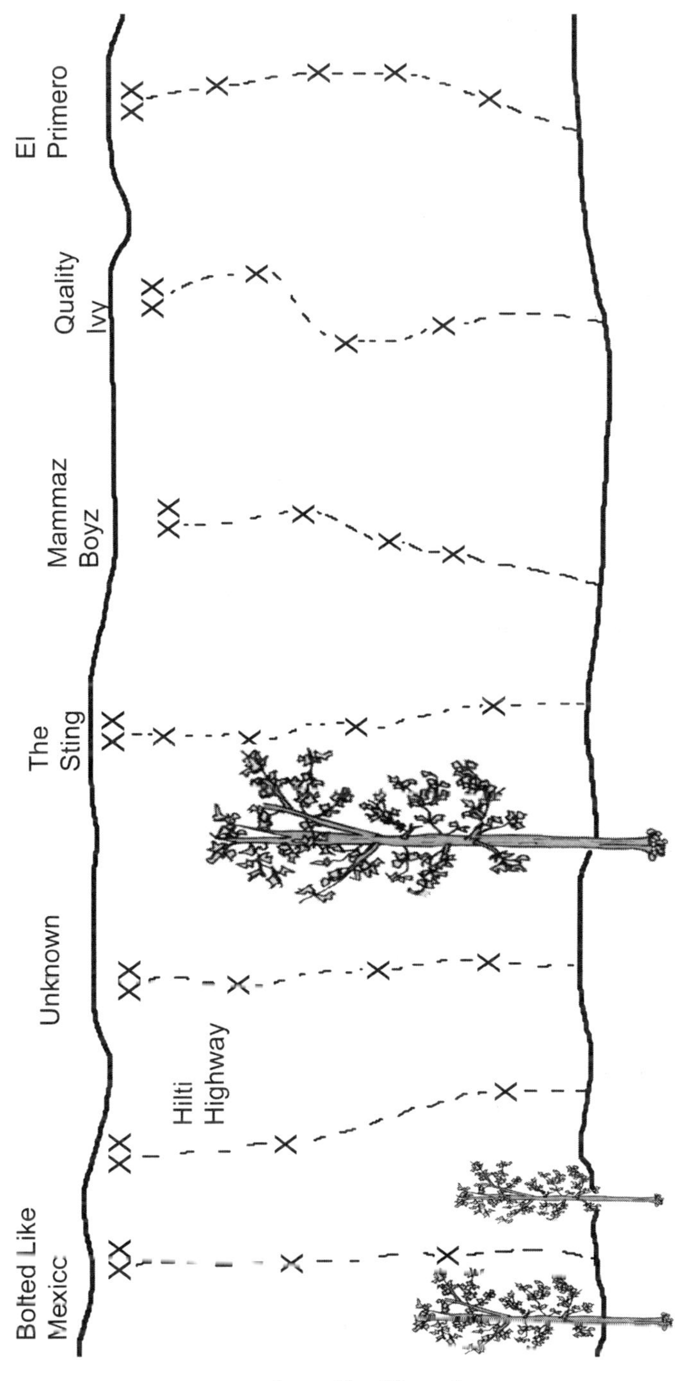

El Primero
Quality Ivy
Mammaz Boyz
The Sting
Unknown
Hilti Highway
Bolted Like Mexicc

5) Unknown (5.10b)

6) Hilti Highway (5.10c)
(FA – Kevin Bentz)

7) Bolted Like Mex (5.10c R)
Starts in front of two trees. It is possible to deck from multiple spots on the route, including the anchors. (FA – Kevin Bentz)

Dead Cat's Wall (right to left)

Dead Cat's Wall is a great beginner and warm-up area. All top rope anchors are now cold shuts, so you just have to run your rope through them and lower. It's the epitome of gym climbing in an outdoor setting. The wall was named after Tom Suhler and Dave Cardosa found a small grave of one of the Reimer's cats called "Emma Peel" close to the wall. The tombstone read "Here lies Emma Peel. She was a good cat."

8) Centipede (5.11a)**
Only the first couple moves are tough. (FA – David Cardosa / Tom Suhler)

9) Power Snatch (5.10c) **
Start off the tufa. Make sustained moves to the top. There is a bit of a run-out to the second bolt. (FA – Jay Stein)

10) Reimerama (5.10a) *
Start right of the large tree. (FA – Scott Hudson)

11) Almost Nothing To It (5.9) *
Start in front of the tree. (FA – Sharon O'Keefe)

12) My Name is Mud (5.9) **
Climb straight up and left of the cave. (FA – Curtis Mai)

AustinRock
ErockOnline.com

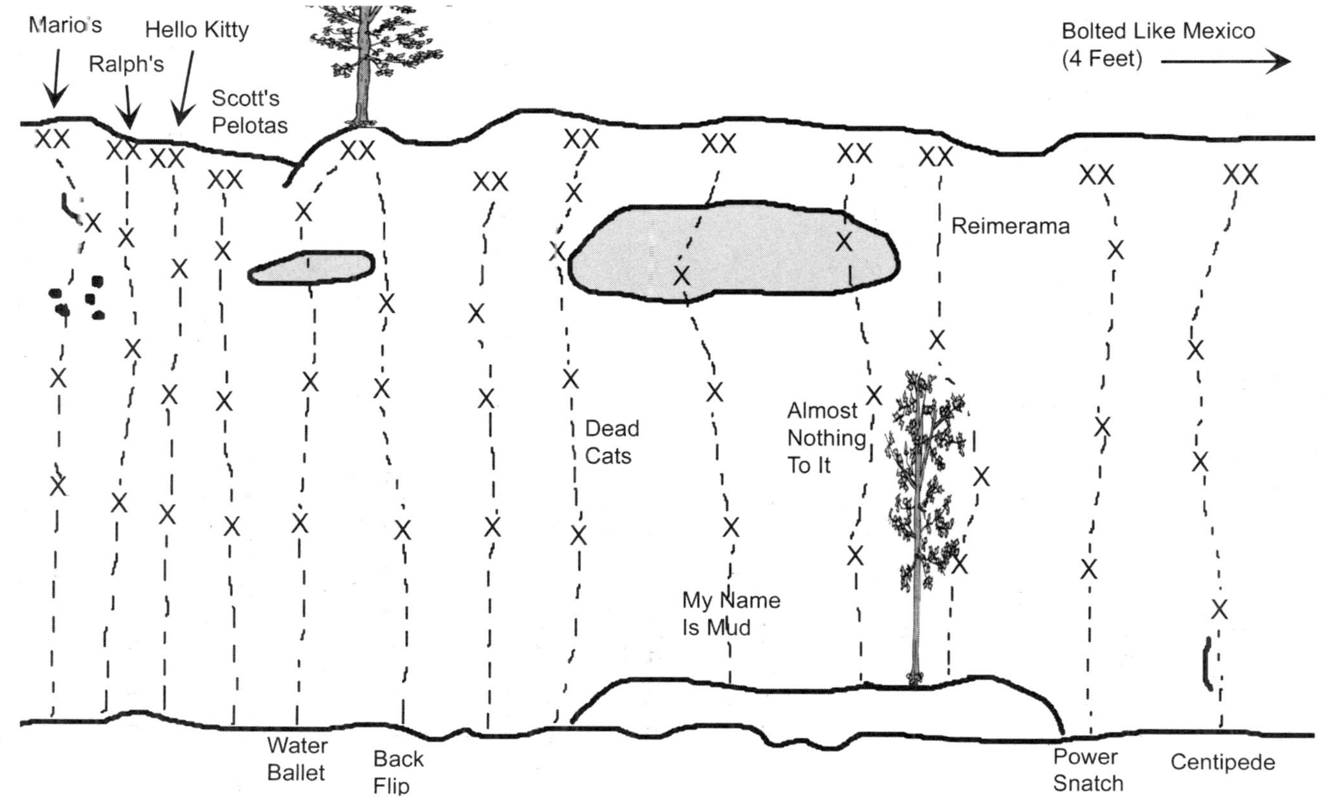

Mario's
Ralph's
Hello Kitty
Scott's Pelotas
Bolted Like Mexico
(4 Feet)
Reimerama
Dead Cats
Almost Nothing To It
My Name Is Mud
Water Ballet
Back Flip
Power Snatch
Centipede

13) Dead Cats Don't Meow (5.10c) **

This was the third route on this wall. The crux of this route is at the top, gaining the anchors. (FA – David Cardosa / Tom Sueler)

14) Backflip (5.9)

The route has its name because of the ease with which the rope gets behind your leg causing you to flip upside down if you fall. (FA – Curtis Mai)

15) Water Ballet (5.10c) *

Climb directly up just left of the obvious water streak. If you climb the water streak directly, the rating is a bit harder. (FA – Scott Hudson)

16) Scott's Pelotas (5.8)

(FA – Scott Hinton)

17) Hello Kitty (5.10a)

(FA – Ralph Vega)

18) Ralph's Route (5.11c)

This route has a hard dead point at the top. (FA – Ralph Vega)

19) Mario's Route (5.12a)*

Easy 5.9 climbing until you get to the bouldery finish. (FA – Mario Cantu)

20) Great Unknown (5.11a)

This route shares the first two bolts with "Smelling Cat Calvin". The anchors are below the cactus. (FA – John Gonzales)

21) Smelling Cat Calvin (5.8)

Start on a vertical face and move left into a dihedral. (3 bolts, 2 top anchors) (FA – Steven Shortnacy)

Tom Suhler bolting "Dead Cats Don't Meow"

22) Clawing Zoë (5.7)
Start right of a small overhang. Climb past a small tree on the right for a sloping finish. (3 bolts, 2 top anchors) (FA – Stephen Shortnacy)

23) Hissing Cloe (5.8)
Start on a lie-back flake left of the small overhang. (3 bolts, 2 top anchors) (FA – Steven Shortnacy)

24) Rolly Poly Cocoa Kitty (5.7) **
(3 bolts, 2 top anchors) (FA – Steven Shortnacy)

25) Lessa the Puramatic 6000 Kitty (5.5) ***
(2 bolts, 2 top anchors) (FA – Steven Shortnacy)

Rhetorick Wall

This is the orange colored wall just left of the Dead Cat's Wall.

1) Punctuation Mark (5.12a)
Climb the featureless water streak and avoid any large hold you may see. Otherwise it's about 5.9. (FA – Rick Watson)

2) Rhetorick (5.12a)
(FA – Rick Watson)

3) Bad Language (5.12a R)
This route climbs through two bolts then moves left, away from the anchors. Why? Who knows.

4) Twyman's Folly (5.12c)
(FA – Matt Twyman)

5) Schizophrenic Calisthenics (5.12d)
(FA – Joe Sulak)

6) The Juice is Loose (V3)
This is behind and below the Rhetorick Wall and traverses an obvious hump in the wall.

Digitron Boulder

1) Digitron (5.10c)
This is the bolted slab on a boulder downhill from the Dead Cats Wall.

a) Traverse Any of the Large Sides (V1)

b) Digitalia (V6)
Climb the Pedernales side of the Digitron Boulder. The landing sucks.

2) T-Rex (5.12a)***
Found on the water side of the large boulder. (FA – John Gonzales)

The Ito Boulder

This boulder is just to the left of "The Juice is Loose" and contains a couple sit start boulder problems.

1) Lance It (V0)
Sit start and climb the arête. Landing sucks.

2) Me Ito (V0)
Sit start to the left of the arête.

The Camachos

These boulders are located next to the Digitron boulder.

The Macho Camacho

1) Rico Camacho (V2)
Sit start on the arête.

2) Buck Camacho (V3)
Sit start to the right of "Rico" and reach the bulge.

3) Rex Camacho (V2)
Sit start to the right of "Buck Camacho".

4) Traverse The Pedernales Slab (V0)

5) Mano Camacho (V0)
This is the crack in the corner.

6) Dedo Camacho (V2)
Sit start the arête. Move left into the finger crack.

The Petit Camacho

1) Suave Camacho (V1)

2) Cool Beans Camacho (V7)

Millennium Wall

This wall has a five foot roof and a starting ledge 15 feet off the ground. It holds the longest clip-up at Reimer's: The Millennium Route. The Millennium Wall is just to the left of the Rhetoric Wall.

1) Rags to Riches (5.11b R)
Rusty pins, loose rock and long run outs. Enjoy! (FA – Scott Hudson)

2) Food Rage (5.13a)

Scott Isgitt bolted this route and so far it has not been sent, at least no one can confirm that it has. It is technically a project. (Bolted by Scott Isgitt, no send as of May 2005)

3) Millennium Traverse (5.10b) **

Start on the 10-foot ledge and traverse right. There are 13 bolts on this route. (2 top anchors) (FA – Mario Cantu)

Arbor Wall

This wall is merely an extension of the Millennium Wall.

4) Mrs. Johnson (5.10b)

(FA – Paul Johnson)

5) Cliptomania (5.11a) **

First bolt is about 15 feet off the ground. This route climbs the blue streak. (2 bolts, 2 top anchors) (FA – Scott Hudson)

6) Arborcidal Tendencies (5.11b) ***

Start in front of a large flat boulder. This route shares some of "Cliptomania". (3 bolts, 2 top anchors) (FA – David Phillips)

7) Deferred Adjudication (5.11b) ***

(FA – David Phillips)

8) George of the Jungle (5.10b)

Start on the face right of the dihedral

9) Ferntasm (5.10b R)

Climb the dihedral in front of the large tree. (2 bolts, 1 piton, 2 top anchors) (FA – Dave and Joey Phillips)

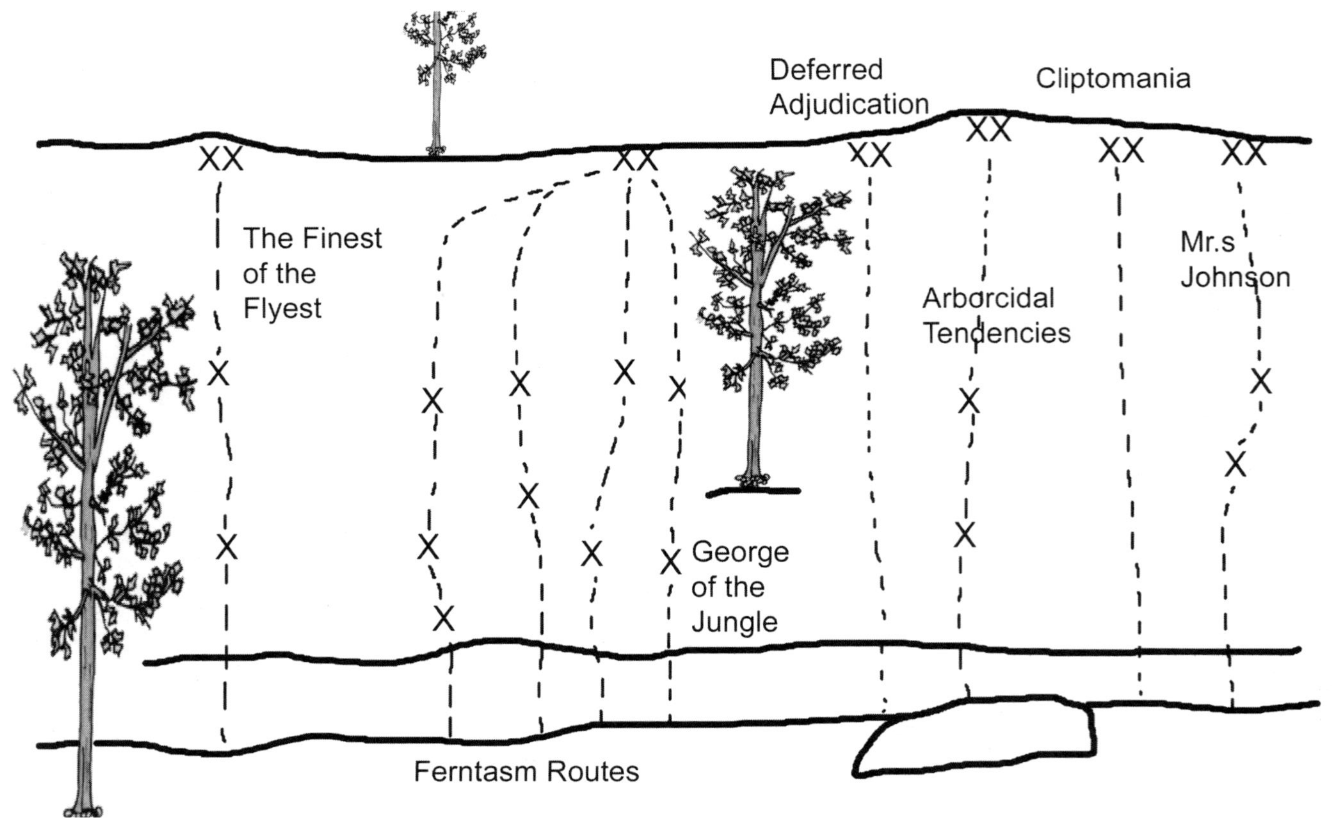

The Finest of the Flyest
Deferred Adjudication
Cliptomania
Arborcidal Tendencies
Mr.s Johnson
George of the Jungle
Ferntasm Routes

10) Left of Ferntasm (5.10b)

This route shares anchors with "Ferntasm". (3 bolts) (FA – Curtis Mai, Todd McCray)

11) Ferntasm Twice Removed (5.11b)

Shares anchors with "Ferntasm". (FA – Curtis Mai, Todd McCray)

12) The Finest of the Flyest (5.11a)

Start on tufa and move to bulging dihedral. (FA – Dave Tekyl)

T-Roofic Wall

This is a great wall that is usually shaded and not very crowded. "T-Roofic" is the prize climb on this wall, and at times may have a line waiting for a ride.

13) Fearless (5.10a)

Climbs the dihedral. If a route could have negative stars, this one would get two or three.

14) Grip Clip (5.12a)

Use "Fearless" anchors. (FA – Jeff Fenaros)

15) Flea Circus (5.11d)

A chipped route with a bit of a run out at the top. (FA – Rick Watson)

16) T-Roofic Detour (5.10d) ***

Climb to the roof and move right following big holds on the orange rock. (FA – Scott Hudson)

17) T-Roofic Direct (5.11b)*****

Begin the climb directly under the second bolt. A stick-clip is a good idea! (FA – Tommy Blackwell)

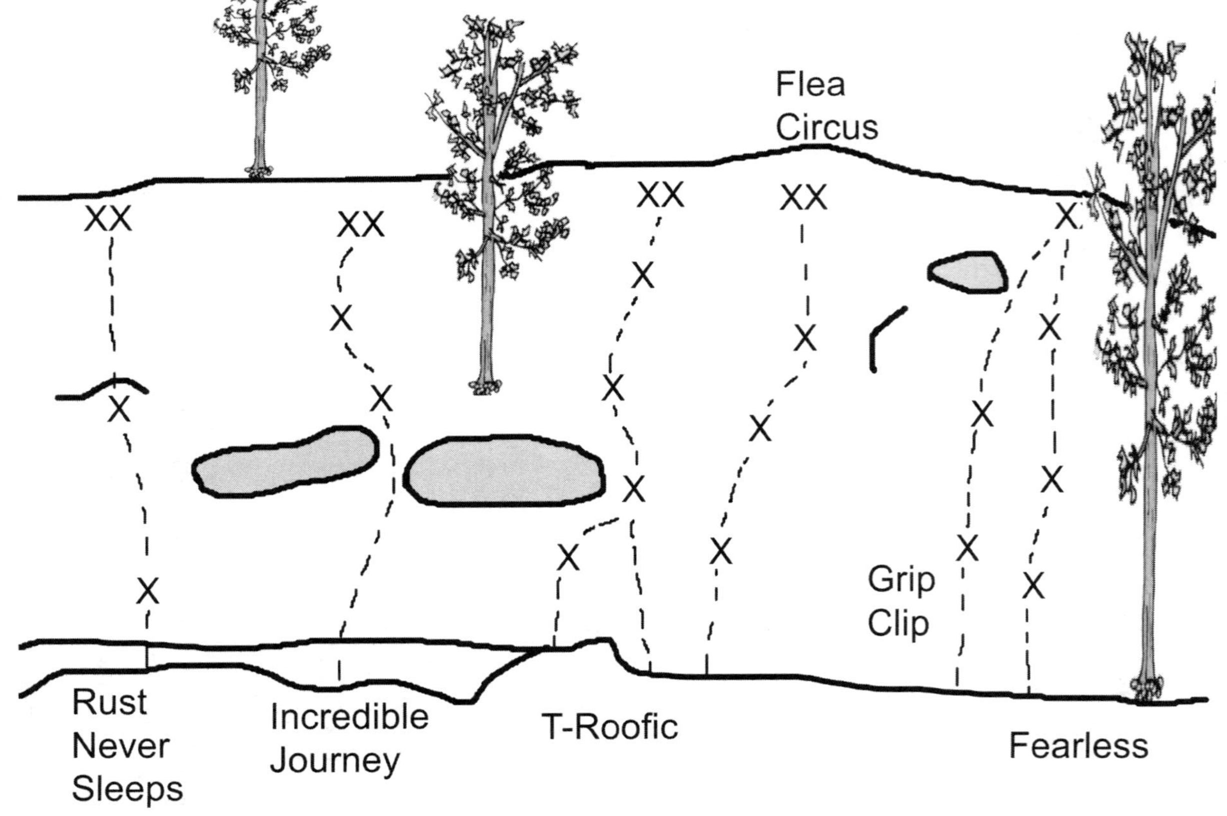

AustinRock
ErockOnline.com

18) Incredible Journey (5.12a) **
Start on the ledge and traverse right under the roof. (FA – Greg Brooks)

19) Rust Never Sleeps (5.12c)
(FA – Jeff Jackson)

20) Nobody's Hero (5.10d) **
This is the grey face. (FA – Benji Fink)

Tit For Tom Wall

Located about 300 yards past the T-Roofic Wall, routes here are generally 5.11 and above.

21) Melt Down (5.12b)
Climb the arête starting from a ledge 10 feet off the ground. (FA – Patrick O'Donnell)

22) Curious George (Lucky's Longy) (5.12a)
Traverse left under the roof. (FA – Mike Klein)

23) Jimmy's Rig (5.12a)
First route left of the roof. (FA – Jimmy Carse)

24) Underdog (5.11a)
(FA – Benji Fink)

25) Antiqua (5.11a)
Climb the roof with a small tree growing from it. There is a large tufa at the bottom, and a flexing block for a crux hold. (FA – John Shannon)

26) Beelzebubba (5.11) ***
(FA – J.D. Fant)

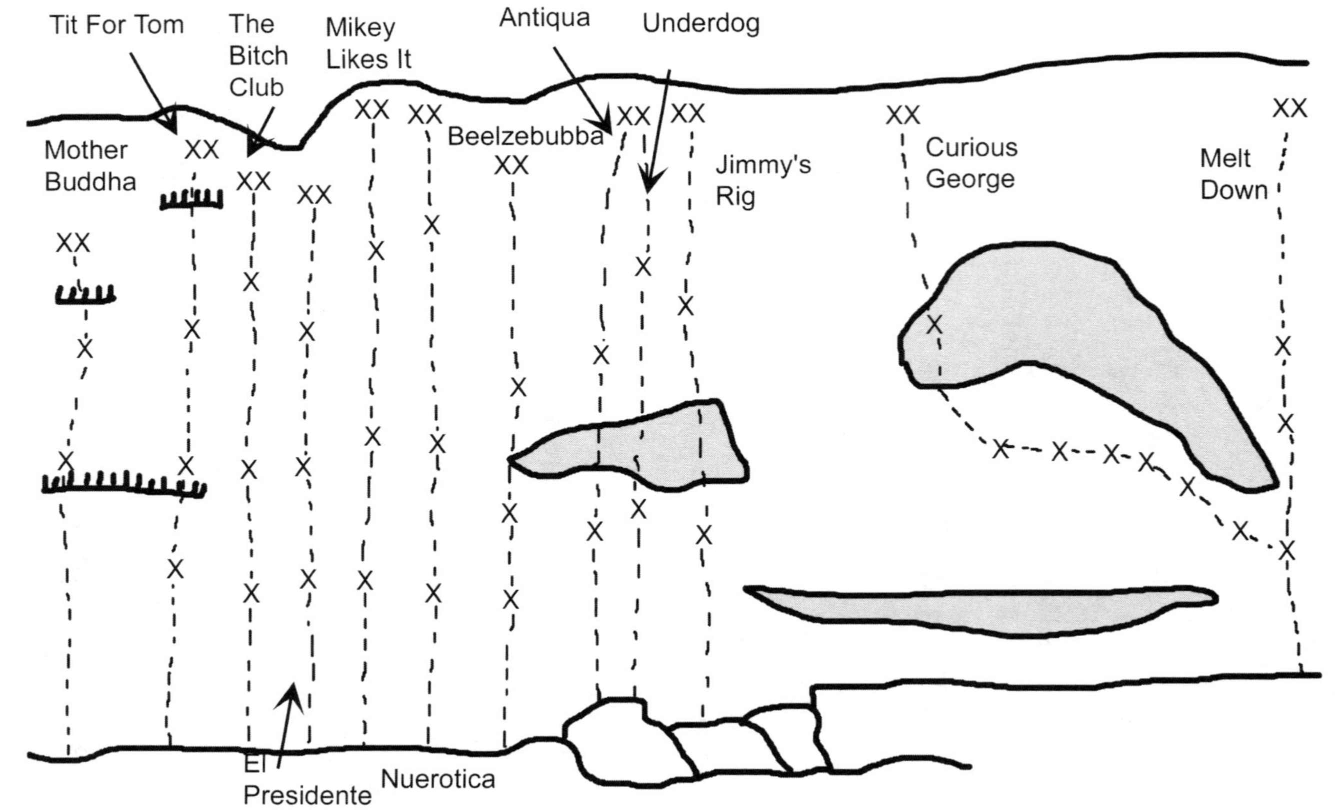

Tit For Tom
The Bitch Club
Mikey Likes It
Antiqua
Underdog
Mother Buddha
Beelzebubba
Jimmy's Rig
Curious George
Melt Down
El Presidente
Nuerotica

Tom Suhler on the first ascent of "Tim For Tom". 1991

27) Nuerotica (5.11d)
Stick-clip the first bolt. One move wonder. 5.9 climbing past bulge. (FA – Joe Sulak)

28) Mikey Likes It (5.10d) **
Climbs the shallow dihedral. (FA – Joe Sulak)

29) El Presidente (5.11a) **
(FA – Rick Watson)

30) The Bitch Club (5.11c)

31) Tit For Tom (5.11c) ***
Start on a lower ramp to gain the higher angles stuff above. (FA – David Cardosa)

32) Mother Buddha (5.11c)
(FA – Clayton Reagan)

Hand Beyond Wall

The Hand Beyond Wall is the last wall on this side. It has several short routes that could be considered high ball boulder problems, but in fact have anywhere from 1 to 4 bolts.

1) Deception Pass (5.10a)*
Climb past the roof to the dihedral (FA – Kevin Bentz)

2) Overlord (5.12b)
(FA – Kevin Bentz)

3) Ten Foot Pole (5.11c)
(FA – Kim Duran)

4) Bluebeard (5.10d)
Large hueco at base of route. (FA – Barry Wilson)

5) Hidden Agenda (5.11b)
Start right of the dihedral. (FA – Kevin Bentz)

6) Antonian (5.9)
There is a run-out to the second bolt.

7) Annie Up (5.6)
Climb the dihedral to the left leaning crack

8) Go For the Jugular (5.9)
Start using the dihedral crack and move to the face. (FA – Kevin Bentz)

9) Monkey Boy (5.10c)
(FA – Kevin Bentz)

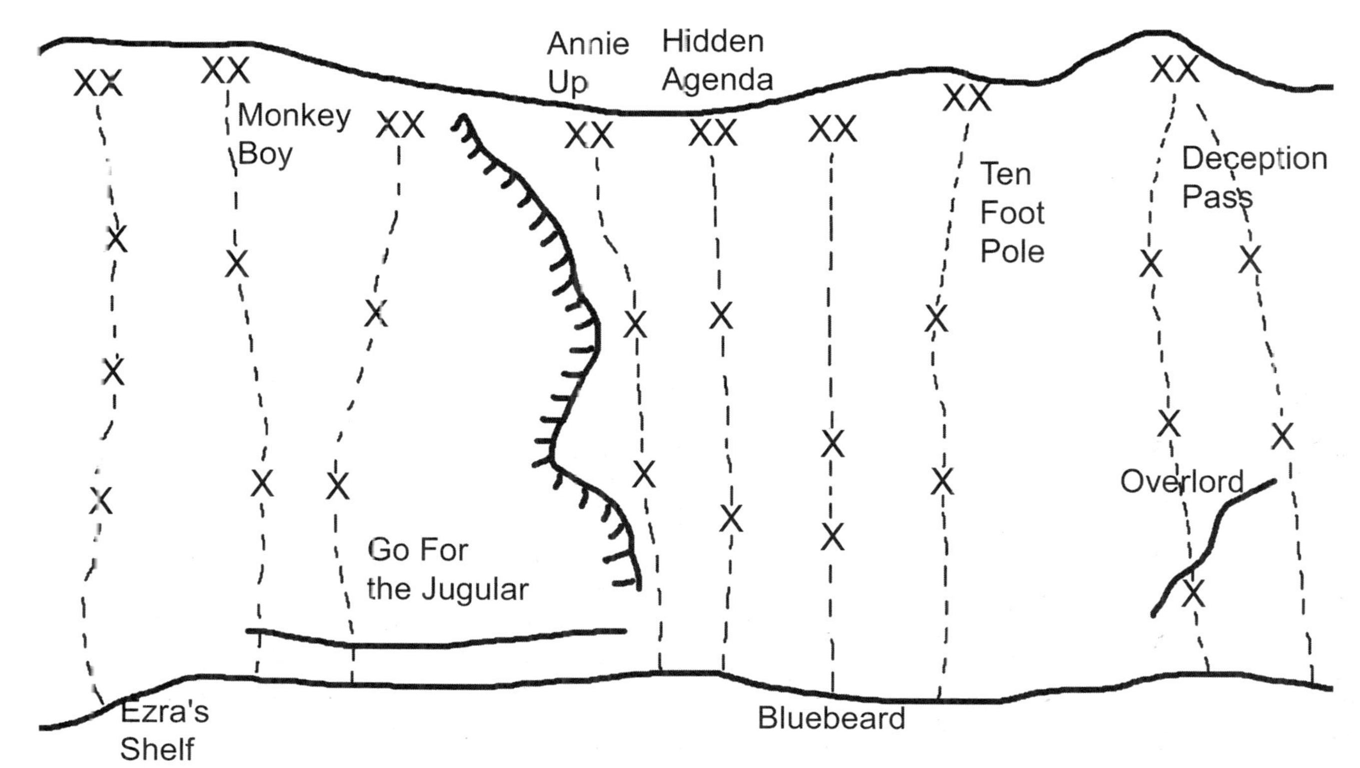

Annie Up
Hidden Agenda
Monkey Boy
Deception Pass
Ten Foot Pole
Go For the Jugular
Overlord
Ezra's Shelf
Bluebeard

10) Ezra's Shelf (5.10d)
Start left of the small tree. (FA – Stephanie Bryant)

11) 5.9

12) Daddy's Girl (5.10b)
Start five feet right of the tree. (FA – Mack Hargrave)

13) Booger Boy (5.10b)
Start next to a leaning tree. (FA – Kevin Bentz)

14) 5.10b
Start using rounded holds

15) Harelipped Dog (5.10b) **
Climb the dihedral and pull the small roof. (FA – Mack Hargrave)

16) San Antonio Drillers (5.10)

17) Power Squat (5.10d)
Start left of the "San Antonio Drillers" dihedral on the arête like thing. (FA – Joe Sulak)

18) Dog on Lag (5.9)

19) Tree Gnome (5.10c)
Start right of large tree

20) Camp Fire Jesus (5.10c)

21) Shadowman (5.11a)
(FA – Kevin Benz)

22) Yet Another S.A. Route (5.10)

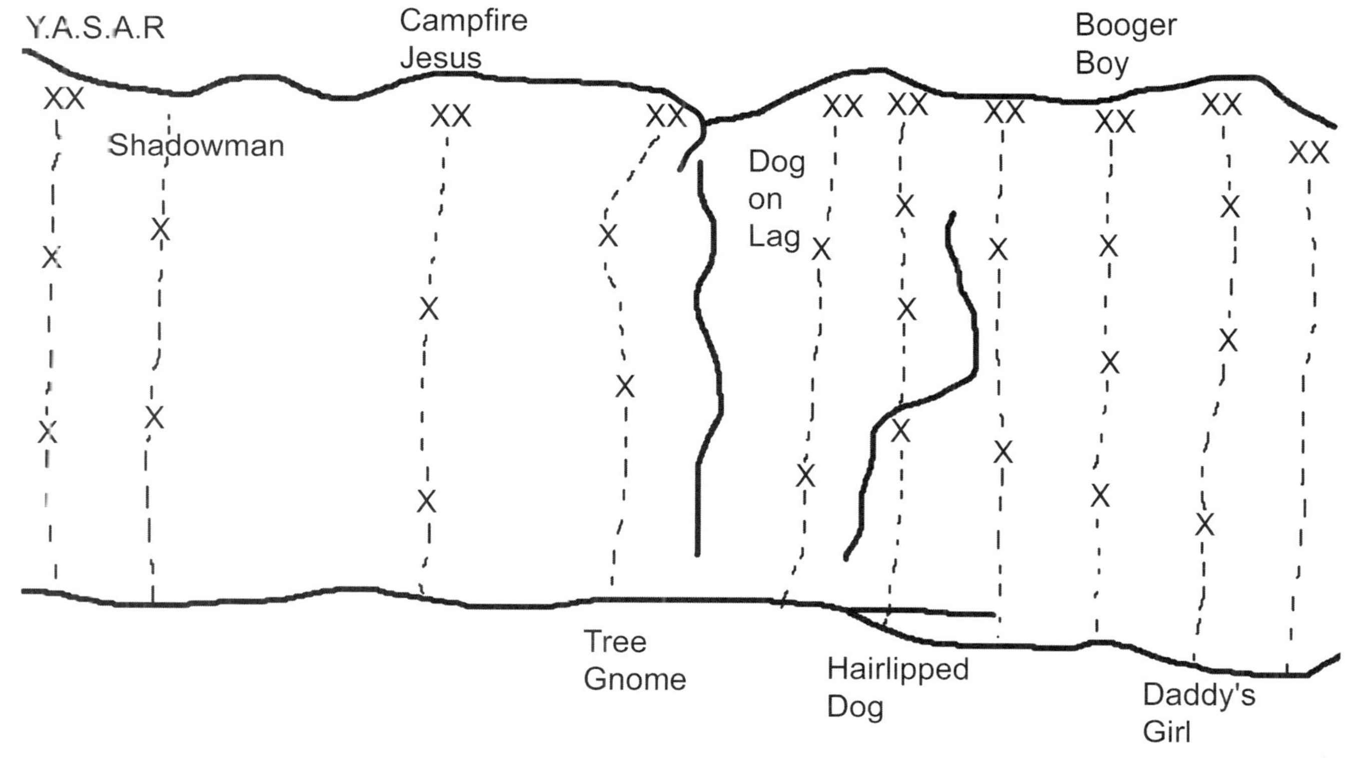

Y.A.S.A.R
Campfire Jesus
Booger Boy
Shadowman
Dog on Lag
Tree Gnome
Hairlipped Dog
Daddy's Girl

World's Greatest Boulder

This is the large boulder close to the water downhill from the T-Roofic Wall. It contains several high quality boulder problems and a couple fine bolted lines as well.

1) Screaming Yellow Zonker's (V1)

2) Pocket Rocket (5.10)
(2 bolts)(FA – Scott Hudson)

3) Size Ain't Shit (5.11c)
(FA – Charlie Chapman)

4) Love Shack (5.12)
(2 bolts)(FA – Paul Clark)

Mike Klein on "Love Shack". www.merrickales.com

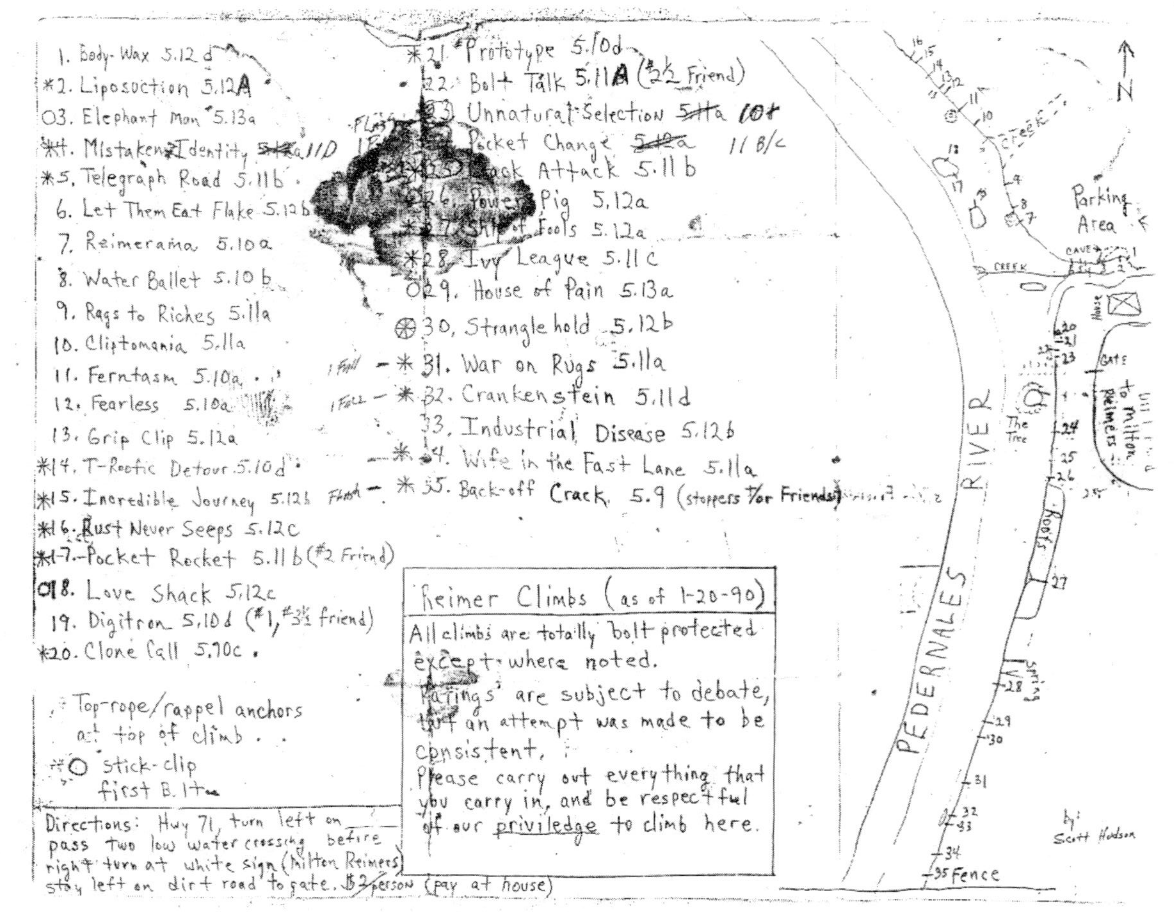

Reimer's First Topo (1990)

AustinRock
ErockOnline.com

Directions:
Go out Highway 71 past the intersection of 620 and 71, then turn left on
Ranch Road 3238 (at the Exxon station, this is the same road that goes
to Hamilton Pool), and continue on that road until you pass two low
water crossings. About one mile after the crossings, turn right at a
white sign for Milton Reimer's ranch. Stay left on the dirt road until
you reach a gate. $2.00 per person - pay at the house.

Ratings are subject to debate, but an attempt was made to be consistent.
All climbs are bolt protected, except where indicated. Please carry out
everything you carry in, and be respectful of our privilege to climb
here.

@ means no anchors at the top of the climb
! means stick clip the first bolt
? means the rating is in doubt
R means runout
Fr means use a friend

Climb Name	Climb Name
1) Spider Grind 5.11B @	27) Pocket Rocket 5.11B (#2 Fr)
2) Body Wax 5.12B/C @	28) Love Shack 5.12C !
3) Head 5.13A @	29) Digitron 5.10D (#1,#3 Fr)
4) Liposuction 5.12A	30) Clone Call 5.10B
5) Elephant Man 5.13? !	31) Mas Cerveza 5.11B
6) Mistaken Identity 5.11D	32) Prototype 5.10C
7) Telegraph Road 5.11C	33) Bolt Talk 5.11B (#2 Fr) @
8) Let Them Eat Flake 5.12?	34) Unnatural Selection 5.11A @
9) Learning To Crawl 5.12B/C	35) Bongo Fury 5.11B @
10) I Never Called You A Beast 5.7	36) Pocket Change 5.12A
11) Maggie's Farm 5.7	37) Crack Attack 5.11B
12) Zoe's First Step 5.0	38) Power Pig 5.12 A/B !
13) Centipede 5.11A	39) Ship Of Fools 5.12A
14) Reimerama 5.10A	40) Ivy League 5.11C
15) Almost Nothing To It 5.9	41) House Of Pain 5.13A !,@
16) Dead Cats 5.10B	42) Rain Dance 5.12B
17) Water Ballet 5.10B	43) Stranglehold 5.12B !
18) Rags To Riches 5.11A	44) Velcro Rodeo 5.12A R
19) Cliptomania 5.11A	45) Ant Encounters 5.11?
20) Ferntasm 5.10B	46) Teenage Parties 5.11A @
21) Fearless 5.10A	47) War On Rugs 5.11A
22) Grip Clip 5.12A	48) Gang Bang 5.11B !
23) T-Roofic Detour 5.10D	49) Crankenstein 5.11C
24) Incredible Journey 5.12B	50) Industrial Disease 5.12B
25) Rust Never Seeps 5.12C	51) Wife In The Fast Lane 5.10D
26) Tit For Tom 5.11B	52) Back Off Crack 5.9 (med-crk Pro)

1

Landfill Wall

The Landfill Wall is the first wall on the opposite side of the canyon from Sex Canyon. It was originally where the Reimer's would throw their big trash such as old sheds they didn't need anymore. This wall is located above the trail before you reach the Suspended Boulder.

1) Pika Peak (5.10)
Directly across the canyon from "Let Them Eat Flake". (3 bolts) (FA – Kevin Bentz)

2) Dos Vatos (5.10d)
To the right of "Pika Peak". (FA – Kevin Bentz)

3) Get Your Fill (5.12a)
(FA – Rupesh Chhagan, Mike Klien)

Teva Slab

This boulder sits by itself below the trail when approaching the Prototype, Shortcake, and Landfill Walls. You can see a one bolt top rope anchor from the trail on top of the boulder. Most of the variations on the face range from 5.6 to 5.10.

Trail Boulder

As you are hiking on your way to the Prototype Wall, you will hike next to this boulder as you round the corner.

1) Traverse Both Sides (V2)

2) The Creek Side (V1)

3) Trail Bend Corner Left (V1)

4) Corner Right (V2)

5) Backside (V0)

Suspended Boulder

As you round the corner of the Trail Boulder, you will see the Suspended Boulder.

1) Suspended Boulder Left (V2)
Start on the lower left portion of the boulder and traverse the hand crack to gain the face.

2) Suspension of Disbelief (V2)
This one starts on the right side.

The Shortcake Wall (AKA Oblivion Wall) (left to right)

To the left of the Prototype and Dr. Seuss Walls. Also known as the Oblivion Wall. All the routes are short, with cruxes at the bottom.

1) Got a Dollar? (5.7)
(FA – Curtis Mai, Todd McCray)

2) Crack Ate The Pipe (5.8)
(FA – Curtis Mai, Todd McCray)

3) Karen Carpenter (5.11)**
This is a three pin route that leads to Fixe clip anchors. (FA – Brenton Buxton, Joel Schopp, and Frank Curry)

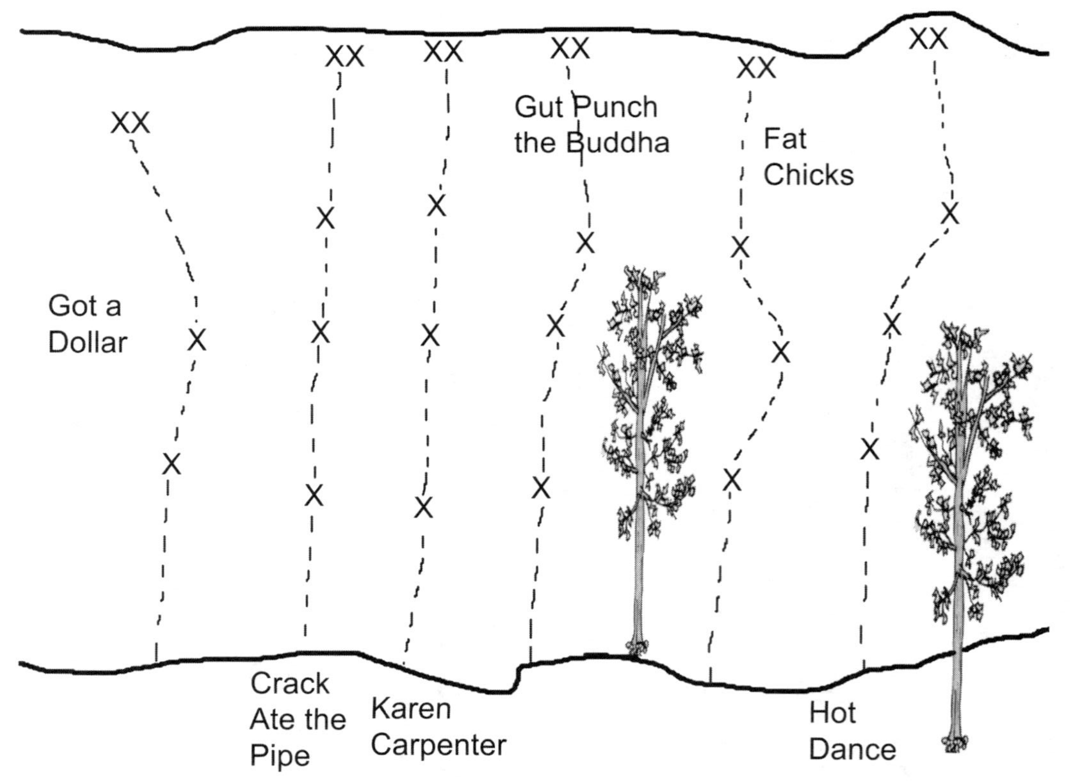
Got a
Dollar
Gut Punch
the Buddha
Fat
Chicks
Crack
Ate the
Pipe
Karen
Carpenter
Hot
Dance

4) Gut Punch the Buddha (5.9)
(FA – Curtis Mai, Todd McCray)

5) Unknown Name (5.11)
(FA – Dave Phillips)

6) Fat Chicks Tryin' To Be Sexy (5.10a)
(FA – Curtis Mai, Todd McCray)

7) Hat Dance (5.9)
Start left of the tree. (FA – Curtis Mai, Todd McCray)

Dr. Seuss Wall

1) Smitten Psychopath (5.9)
Climb the left end of the roof up a poorly protected face. The first bolt becomes useless very fast, as it is a bit low to be very effective. (3 bolts, 2 top anchors) (FA – Curtis Mai)

2) Buttered Side Up (5.11c)
(FA – Josh Pierce)

3) Star Belly Sneech (5.10c)
Climb the right side of the roof.

4) Toilet Solo (5.9)
This route has no bolts. (FA – Josh Pierce)

5) Socks On Chicks (5.10c)**
Climb the face to the left of the tree. This route is stiff because route finding is a bit of a challenge. (FA – Todd McCray)

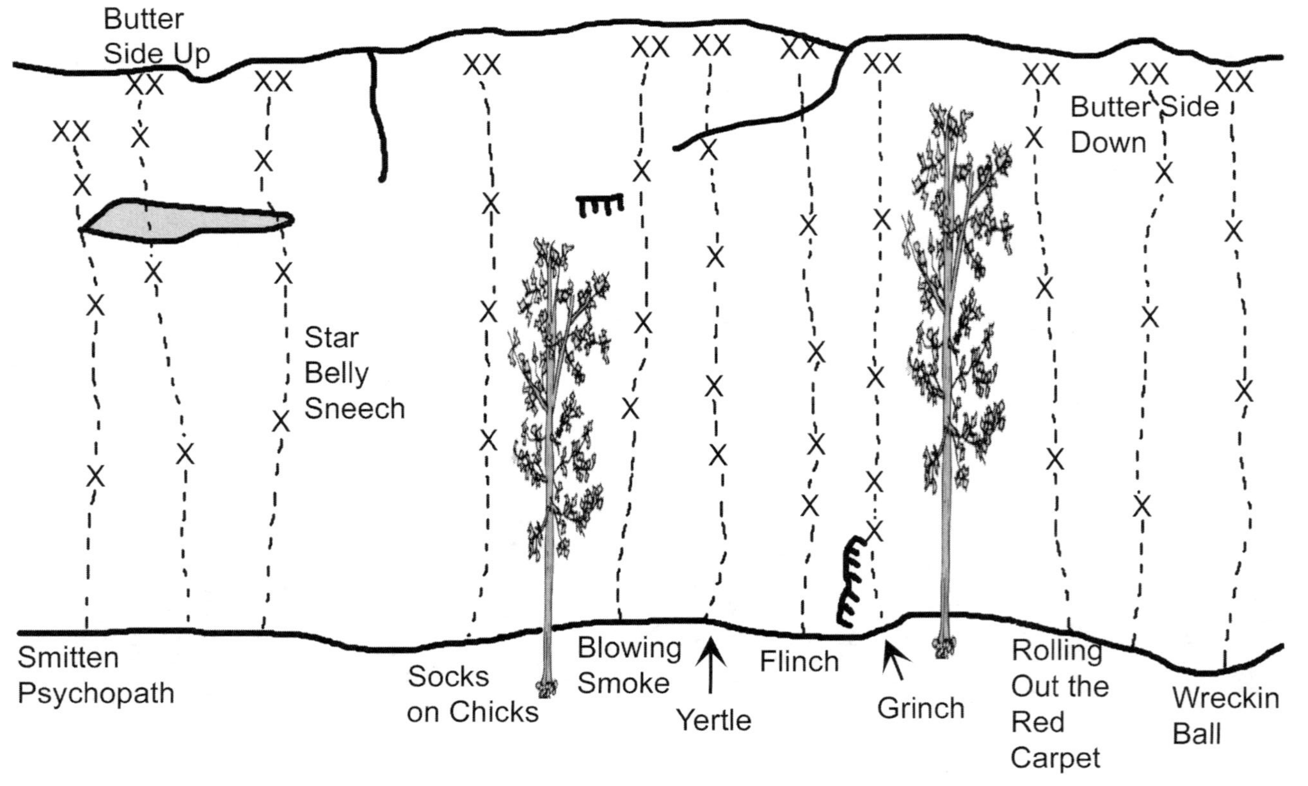

AustinRock
ErockOnline.com

6) Blowing Smoke At the Monkey (5.11a)***
To the right of the tree is this fantastic route. Make the fun sequence to the first bolt and then choose to go directly to the second, or by moving left slightly to the second bolt. A bold section above and another bolt will see you to the anchors. Watch out for the poison ivy to the left by the ledge! (3 bolts, 2 top anchors) (FA – Curtis Mai)

7) Yertle The Turtle (5.12a)***
Climb the face in front of the tree following a few good rails and a couple hard to reach pockets. Super great route! (4 bolts, 2 top anchors)

8) Flinch (5.12b)***
This is very powerful route next to "Yertle". The fourth clip is a booger!

9) Grinch (5.12c)***
Start to the left of the tree off the flake. Classic moves on this one.

10) Rolling Out the Red Carpet (5.12b)
Start to the right of the tree. (FA – Rupesh Chhagan)

11) Buttered Side Down (5.11b)
Uses a horizontal crack. (FA – Josh Pierce)

12) Wreckin' Ball (5.12a)
Use a medium sized crack

Prototype Wall

The Prototype Wall is an often crowded warm-up spot and the mix of climbers and their dogs can make for cacophonous outing. Super classic routes riddle the wall which makes the wait worth it.

1) 8 Flake (5.8)***

The usual warm-up for many parties that climb on this wall. Follow the obvious sweeping crack found on the left side of the wall. (5 bolts, 2 top anchors)

2) Bisector (5.10a)

Climb the face directly below the "8 Flake" anchors (FA – Curtis Mai)

3) Clone Call (5.9)

Climb the dihedral to the "8 Flake" anchors. (FA – Scott Hudson)

4) Damasiadas Cervezas (5.12a)**

This is the bolted line immediately right of "Clone Call". The top is burly!! (3 bolts, 2 top anchors) (FA – Scott Isgitt, Scott Steiner)

5) Mas Cerveza (5.11b)***

This is the route that runs parallel to "Prototype". The opening moves are tweaky and sharp. (5 bolts, 2 top anchors) (FA – Rick Watson)

6) Prototype (5.10d)***

This is the usual warm-up for the usual crowd. Climb up to the starting perch and clip the first bolt. Follow fun climbing up through a combination of small pockets and huge jugs all the way to the anchors. An absolute must do! (5 bolts, 2 top anchors) (FA – Jean and Scott Hudson)

7) Sugar (5.10d)

8) Bolt Talk (5.11a)***

(FA – Jean Hudson)

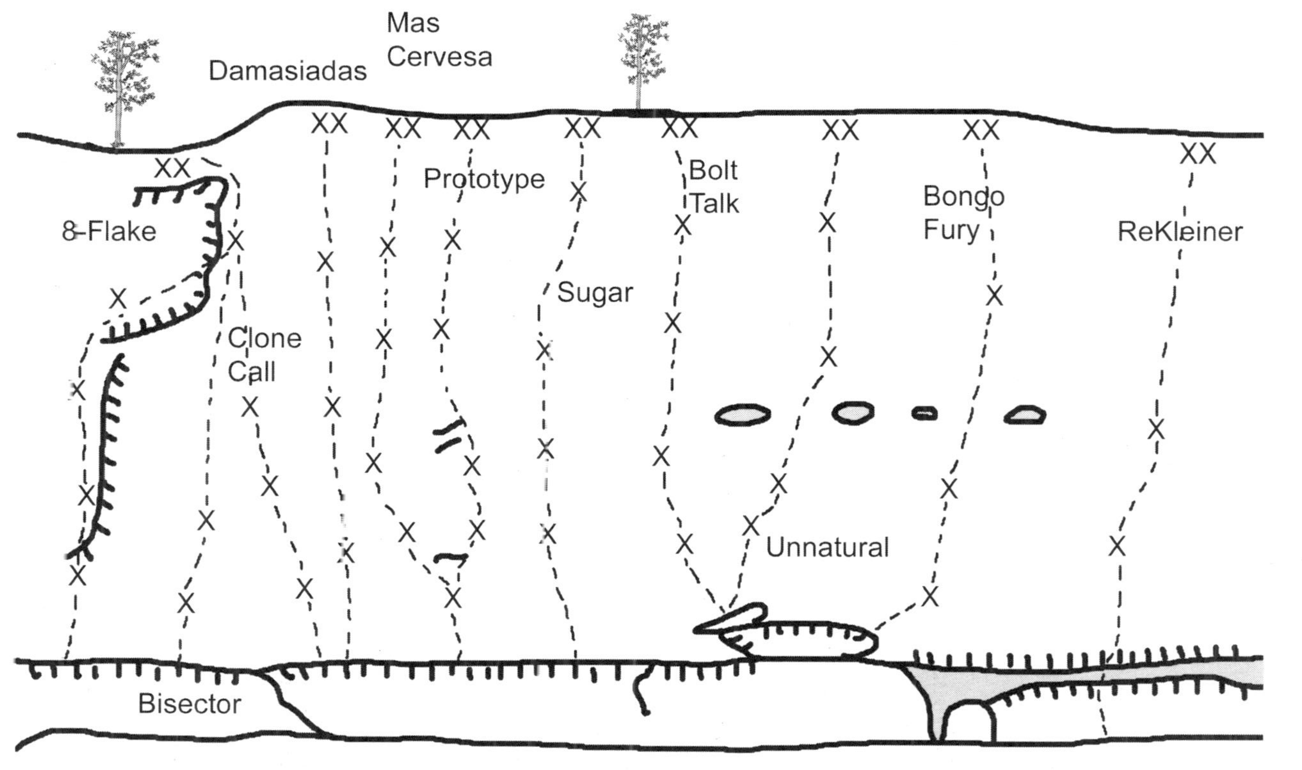
Damasiadas
Mas Cervesa
8-Flake
Prototype
Bolt Talk
Bongo Fury
ReKleiner
Clone Call
Sugar
Unnatural
Bisector

9) Unnatural Selection (5.11a)**
Start this route from the left side of the balanced boulder. The holds are small, but the feet are good, making this an excellent route. Fairly run-out between the second and third bolts, but with big holds to clip from. (4 bolts, 2 top anchors w/ chains) (FA – Jean and Scott Hudson)

10) Bongo Fury (5.11c)***
Start off the high boulder. (FA – Rick Watson)

11) Bongo Direct (5.13)
Start from the ground.

12) The ReKleiner (5.13b)
(FA – Rupesh Chhagan, Mike Klien)

Blue Lizard Boulder

This is the large boulder downhill from Prototype Wall close to the water.

1) Traverse Left to Right and Reverse (V1)

2) The Blue Lizard (V2)

3) Ped Side (V0-2)

Mai Tai Wall

This wall is to the right of the Prototype Wall marked by the tree on the ledge.

1) Mai Type (5.10)
This is the first route, just left of the tree. There is a bit of run-out to the anchors.

2) Tree (5.9)***
A great route with a variety of climbing techniques involved in the ascent. Start on the ledge next to the big tree.

3) Mega Lounge (5.8)
(FA – Curtis Mai)

4) Let the Wallies Loose (5.9)
(FA – Curtis Mai)

5) I Speak For the Trees (5.10a)
(FA – Curtis Mai)

6) Crack Smack (5.9)
(FA – Curtis Mai, Todd McCray)

7) Herbivore Connoisseur (5.11a)
(FA – Rupesh Chhagan)

8) Unknown

9) Check Your Head (5.12c)
(FA – Rupesh Chhagan)

10) Swingers (5.12d)
Bolted by Kirk Jones and Marisa Hinton. (FA – Rupesh Chhagan)

Insect Wall

1) Pocket Change (5.10d)
(FA – Scott Hudson)

2) Crack Attack (5.10d)
(FA – Jean Hudson)

3) Three Slackateers (5.11c)
(FA – Rupesh Chhagan, Bonner Armbruster, Maris Hinton)

4) Power Pig (5.12b)
(FA – Christina Jackson)

5) Deflower Power (5.12a/b)
Named because a tree was cut down in order to set this route. (FA – Rupesh Chhagan, James Harrison)

6) Dragonfly (5.12d)
(FA – Wayne Crill)

7) Malaria (5.13a)
(FA – Mike Klein)

8) Mantis (5.13b)
(FA – Rupesh Chhagan, James Harrison)

9) Scorpion Child (5.12c)***
Marked by the black tufa on the headwall. Start from a super dynamic roof at the bottom, to a tufa pinching middle, to a thin face at the top. (FA – James Harrison)

10) Wild Spider (5.13c)
(FA – Mike Klein)

11) Reptile (project)

12) Alip (5.13b)
(FA – Matt Twyman)

13) Rotten Oasis (5.13c/d)
(FA – Rupesh Chhagan)

14) Backslider Direct (5.12d)

Start left of the "Backslider" start and climb straight into the "Backslider" finish. (FA – Rupesh Chhagan)

15) Backslider (5.12c)

16) Singularity (5.13a)

(FA – Matt Twyman)

17) Stickbug (5.13d)

(FA – Rupesh Chhagan, Mike Klein)

18) Cinching Up the Rootlock (5.13d)

(FA – Rupesh Chhagan)

19) Dreamkeeper (5.13b)

(FA – Mike Klein, Jeff Jackson, Clayton Reagan, Rupesh Chhagan)

20) Brainstem (5.14a)

This route starts with a serious move to a gaston. Cut left to finish "Dreamkeeper". (FA – Rupesh Chhagan, Clayton Reagan)

21) Evolution of Choss (5.14a)

Start on "Brainstem". Go right and finish on "Too Many Donuts". (FA – Clayton Reagan)

22) Too Many Donuts (5.11)

This is the bolt line to the left of "Ship of Fools". (FA – Mike Klein)

23) Ship of Fools (5.12a)

This route starts on the ramp to the left of the roofs. Watch for the beehive. (FA – Russell Rand)

24) Block Party (5.13a)***
This climb traverses the roof 100 yards left of "Jade". Follow straightforward climbing to the roof. Traversing the roof requires several strenuous moves and many heel hooks. All bolts are perma-hung with draws. (FA – Mike Klein)

House of Pain

The House of Pain Wall is packed full of relatively hard routes and is generally where you will find Austin's hard core hanging out. Many of the routes have high first bolts, and a couple start off cheater stones. A stick clip is a good idea here. Nearly all routes are of super quality.

1) Ivy League (5.11b)
The poison ivy on this routes gets cleaned from time to time, but beware, it could be there when you climb it. (FA – Russell Rand)

2) Bastard in the Brothel (5.11a)
Climb the dihedral and traverse left of the roof to the face. (FA – Rupesh Chhagan)

3) Catharsis Roof (5.12c)***
Start as with "Jade" through the first 5 bolts on 5.11c/d terrain and begin the tough sequence up and slightly left to the bolt in the roof above. This is run-out, but the fall is super clean! Once you clip the last bolt, the crux begins as you climb through thin holds to get over the roof. (6 bolts, 2 top anchors w/ chains) (FA – Rupesh Chhagan)

Hire a qualified guide to this area at Rock-About.com

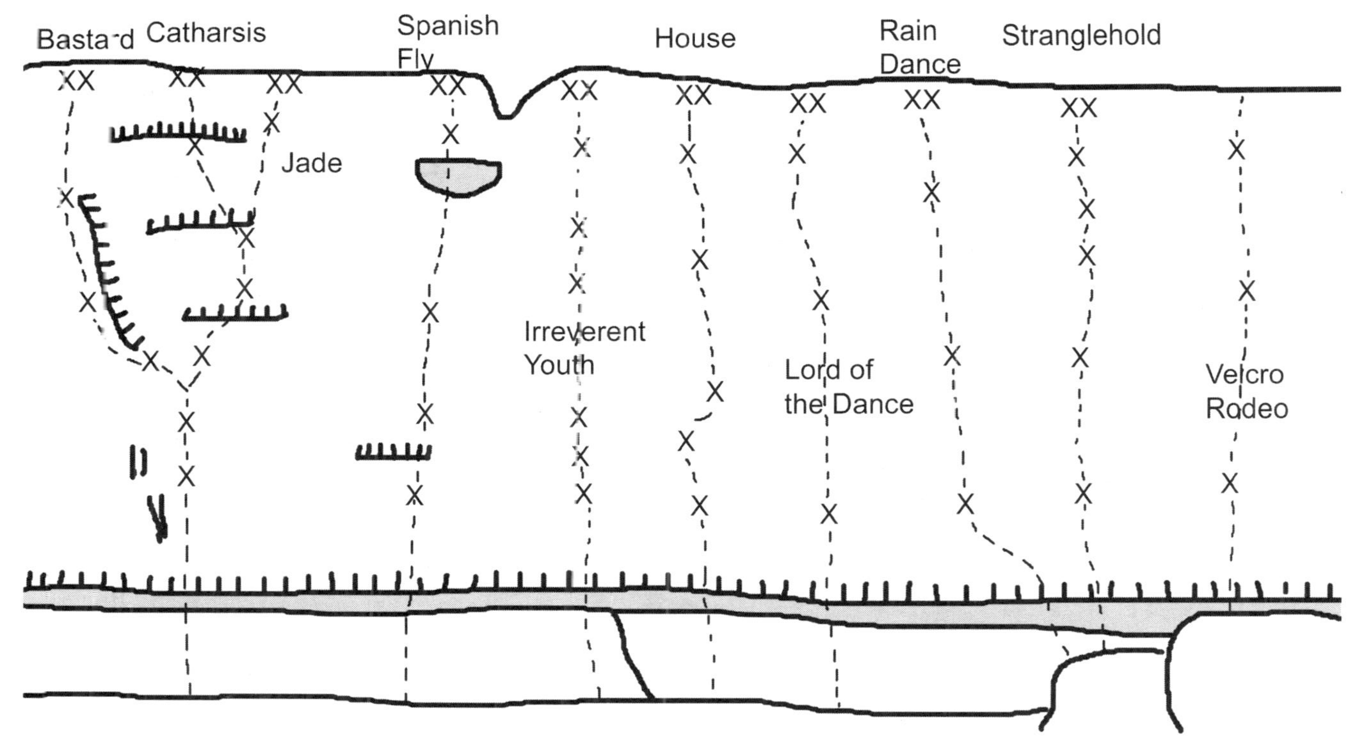

Basta-d Catharsis
Spanish Fly
House
Rain Dance
Stranglehold
Jade
Irreverent Youth
Lord of the Dance
Velcro Rodeo

Nick Douglas on "Irreverent Youth". Merrickales.com

4) Jade (5.12a/b)***

An ultra classic route that starts with climbing through tufa. Follow fun climbing with good protection through 5 bolts. Once over the first roof, move right on big holds to gain the last bolt. The route is run-out here, but the fall is all air and is generally a requirement when projecting. (6 bolts, 2 top anchors w/ chains) (FA – Mike Klein)

5) Angular Momentum (5.11c)

Start on "Jade" and traverse below the roof following the bolts right to the last bolt of "Spanish Fly". Finish to the chains to the right of "Spanish Fly". (FA – Karl Guthrie)

6) Spanish Fly (5.12c)

(FA – James Harrison)

7) Irreverent Youth (5.13d)**

This is quit possibly one of the first lines of it's grade in Central Texas. (FA – Clayton Reagan)

8) Irreverent Spoof (5.14a)

Eliminate the House of Pain rest as with "Irreverent Youth". (FA – Rupesh Chhagan)

9) House of Pain (5.13a)***

This is another of a list of classics on the wall, and the namesake for the entire section of rock. There is a drilled pocket low on the route. Eliminate that, and it's said to be a couple letter grades harder. (FA – Jeff Jackson)

10) Lord of the Dance (5.13a)

(FA – Matt Twyman)

Zach on "Rain Dance". www.merrickales.com

AustinRock
ErockOnline.com

11) Rain Dance (5.12b)***

Start off the boulder and traverse left. Stick-clip the first bolt unless you are sure you will make it. (4 bolts, 2 top anchors) (FA – Russell Rand)

12) Stranglehold (5.12b)***

Start off the boulder as with "Rain Dance". Grab two crimps and begin the series of moves to gain a rest stance by the second bolt. (Don't blow the second clip!) Stick clip the first bolt. (5 bolts, 2 top anchors) (FA – Greg Brooks)

13) Velcro Rodeo (5.12a R)

(FA – Jeff Jackson)

Crankenstein Wall

1) Pearl (5.11c)

(FA – Mike Klein)

2) Natural (5.10c)*

(AKA – Sunday Mass) Start off two crimpers to rock up to the hueco and get a good clipping stance. Follow jugs and ledges to the anchors. (3 bolts, 2 top anchors w/ chains)

3) Ant Encounters (5.11a)

(FA – Tom Suhler)

4) Unknown

5) Unknown

6) Die Hard (5.10a) **

This route is in the obvious dihedral to the left of a small tree. Make an interesting couple of moves to gain the first bolt. (4 bolts, 2 top anchors w/ chains) (FA – Luke Bowman, Tommy Blackwell, Evan Jackson)

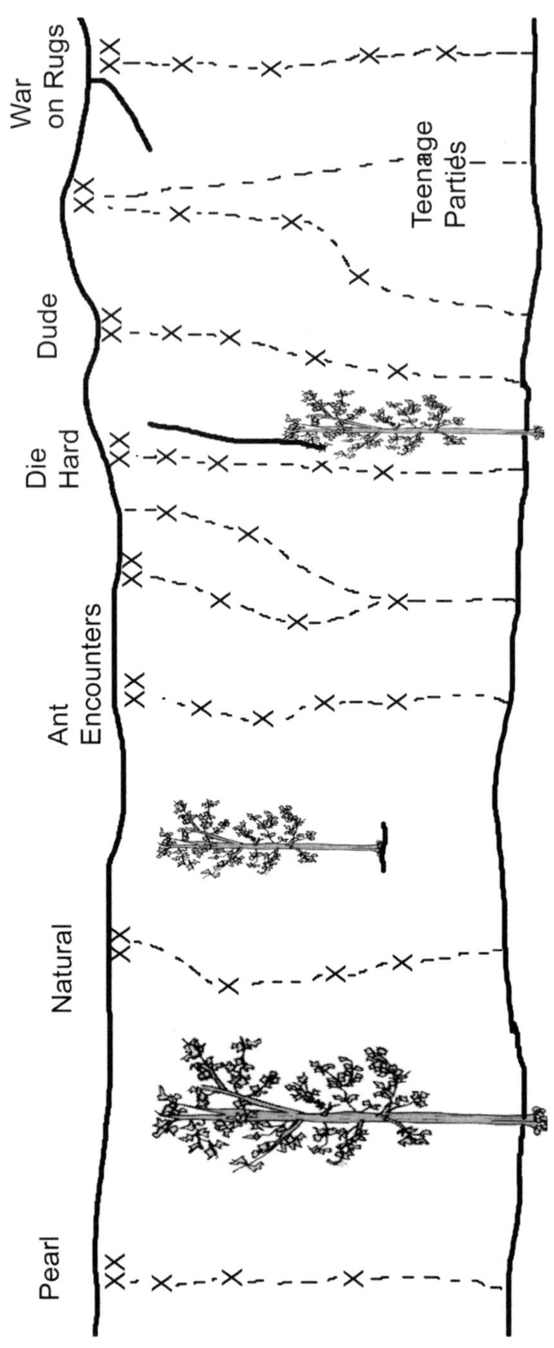

AustinRock
ErockOnline.com

7) Dude, Where's My Hammer (5.11b)**
A balancey crimpy high foot start sets the tone for this bit of Austin sweetness. The finish is less than obvious. An onsite on this line is a credit to any climber. (4 bolts, 2 top anchors w/ chains) (FA – Luke Bowman, Tommy Blackwell, Evan Jackson)

8) Unknown

9) Teenage Parties (5.11b)
The roof start is difficult. (FA – Rick Watson)

10) War on Rugs (5.10d) **
Fun start with a good finish. (FA – Scott Hudson)

11) More Wasabi (5.12c)
Real serious beginning. The fun isn't done till you hit the top. (FA – Karl Guthrie)

12) You Bet Arête (5.11c)
Start through chossy dihedral. (FA – Kevin Gallagher)

13) Santeria (5.11c)
Start on "Gang Bang". Move left after the dyno

14) Gang Bang (5.11a)***
This route gets its rating from the first few moves. Start off the man made cairn pile to grab a great starting hold. Pull the bottom crux section to gain easier ground above. The pump sticks with you to the top. Stick clip the first bolt. There was once a large boulder where the cairn pile is, so it's not cheating if you use it. (FA – Jeff Jackson)

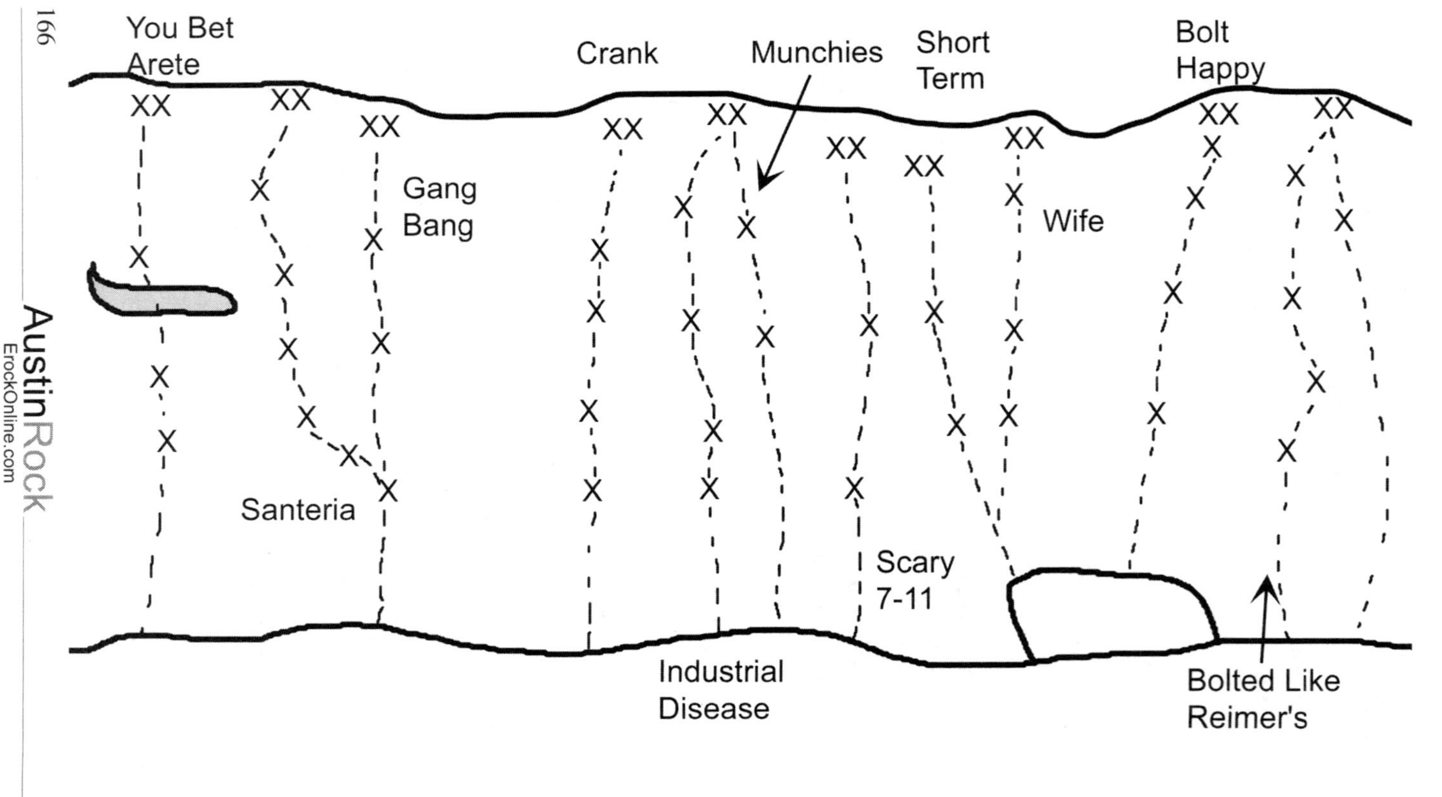

You Bet Arete
Crank
Munchies
Short Term
Bolt Happy
Gang Bang
Wife
Santeria
Scary 7-11
Industrial Disease
Bolted Like Reimer's

15) Bride of Crankenstein (5.11b)
(FA – Karl Guthrie)

16) Crankenstein (5.11c/d)***
(FA – Scott Hudson)

17) Industrial Disease (5.12b)
Pulls through a small roof. (FA – Greg Brooks)

18) The Munchies (5.11c)
(FA – Paul Irby)

19) Scary 7-11 (5.10)
Climb large crack system full of poison ivy

20) Short Term Memory Loss (5.11c)
Starts using the first bolt of "Wife". (FA – Rick Watson)

21) Wife in the Fast Lane (5.10d)***
(FA – Jean Hudson)

22) Bolt Happy (5.11d)
Start off the boulder. Traverse the ramp to the fourth bolt. (FA – Dave Phillips)

23) Bolted Like Reimers (5.10b)
Climb the face left of the crack. (FA – Steven Shortnacy)

24) Back Off Crack (5.9)
Trad gear required. There is one bolt on it. (FA – Injinio Jones)

Dude, Where's My Hammer?

In 2004 most of the obvious lines at Reimer's Ranch had been located and bolted. So when Luke Bowman had spied out an unclimbed route that finished in a sweet dihedral, we were pumped about the chance to put up something new.

Tommy Blackwell. Photo by J. Beveridge

His route is located on the far right band of cliffs at Reimer's, between **"Ant Encounters"** (near the House of Pain wall) and **"Teenage Parties"** on the War on Rugs Wall. He decided to call it **"Die Hard"**, rated at 5.10.

Luke, Evan Jackson and I humped our gear the three quarter's of a mile to the route. While we were working on putting in the hardware, we noticed another possible line just 10 feet to the right, so after finishing **"Die Hard"**, we top roped this other line to see if it was worth bolting. It was! It has an interesting start to a not so obvious finish. It would make a fine 5.11.

As we didn't have enough hardware to bolt it that day, we stood at the base and made plans to come back. We also asked each other what it should be called. We expressed the usual stupid names. None seemed to have any character. Then a girl (whose identity shall remain shrouded in secrecy) climbing near us offered an idea for a name.

She said: Your new climb will be located between **"Teenage Parties"** and **"Die Hard"**. Why don't you call it **"Teenage Hard-Ons"**! We were stunned. It was the perfect name! We thanked her and finished our day.

Later in the week, Luke or I created a post about "another new route" at Reimer's. We espoused all about **"Teenage Hard-Ons"**, where it was located, how hard it was rated, number of bolts it would have, how it got its name and blah blah blah. I can be "Mr. Blah Blah" and probably went overboard talking about it.

So it shouldn't have been any surprise when other folks began to post about how the name was "obscene" and they take their children to these climbing areas and we should have better names and that they will never climb the route, and on and on.

Over the next few days the post turned into a discussion about other route names and what was obscene anyway? Luke and I stuck to our guns, this **"Teenage Hard-Ons"** wasn't so bad compared to other route names and besides, it was a good fit.

A few weeks later we got our gear together and the three of us headed in to bolt it. We got the chains set, then worked the route to assure our selves we had selected the best bolt positions, put in the 4 bolts and began the process of cleaning the route of loose rock and debris. The next thing we knew, I couldn't find the hammer. Misplacing a tool or piece of gear during such an operation isn't unusual. We each carry in our usual climbing gear plus all the additional tools and tool bags, the drill and extra batteries, additional slings and webbing and extra ropes. So the hammer was just under one of the packs or tarps laying on the ground.

No big deal, while Evan and Luke worked to define the best sequences on the route I looked for the hammer. I remembered that Evan was the last to use it. He had been dinging a soft piece of rock near the anchors. I asked him if he knew where the hammer was. He looked at his harness and then at me and said he wasn't sure where it was. Maybe it was near his pack. I looked in his pack, under his pack, in all of our packs, under everything on the ground, behind the rocks. Dang! Then, it dawned on me. We had lots of friends nearby watching our progress. They were climbing **"House of Pain"** just to our left, or had walked by to climb **"War on Rugs"** or the more popular **"Crankenstien"** just 200 feet to the right. One of our friends must be playing a joke on us.

I walked over the one group and politely asked if the knew the location of our hammer. They denied any knowledge. I asked another group and then another. All denied it. I went back and

looked through our gear, again. Nothing. I went back to our friends and looked through their gear.

After about 2 and half hours I was stumped. I knew that something as large and heavy as a hammer with 24" runner and locking carabiner hadn't just walked off. But it wasn't here.

We have a friendly group in Austin, but I was beginning to get on everyone's nerves. I had already asked twice, now I was asking again. Most didn't even answer, they just shook their heads, as I walked near them.

Evan finally spotted it 25 feet off the ground hanging by its runner in a tree below the anchors. The runner was green and the hammer had a grey handle with black head, it had blended in.

It was obvious what had happened. The last time that Evan had used the hammer, we had lowered him through the branches of the tree. The tree had somehow stripped the hammer from his harness and unclipped the carabiner and snagged the hammer.

We were glad to find it, it had been a vexing problem and mostly our friends were glad that I would quit bothering them about it. We knew we had a new name for the route.

Allen Peters on "Queer Junkies". www.merrickales.com

McKinney Falls State Park

From I-35, take exit 230B and go east on Ben White (Hwy 71). After about a mile take a right on Burleson. Veer left to stay on Burleson. Drive about 3 miles and turn right on McKinney Falls Rd. Drive for about 2 miles and turn right into the park. Pay $2 to get in (or with a Texas Conservation Passport you get in free - $60). Drive in and take the first right; park at the dead end. Walk down the dirt road and veer left over to the huge limestone slab until you find the approach tree (tree with a branch leaning against the wall for easy access). All walls described from left to right.

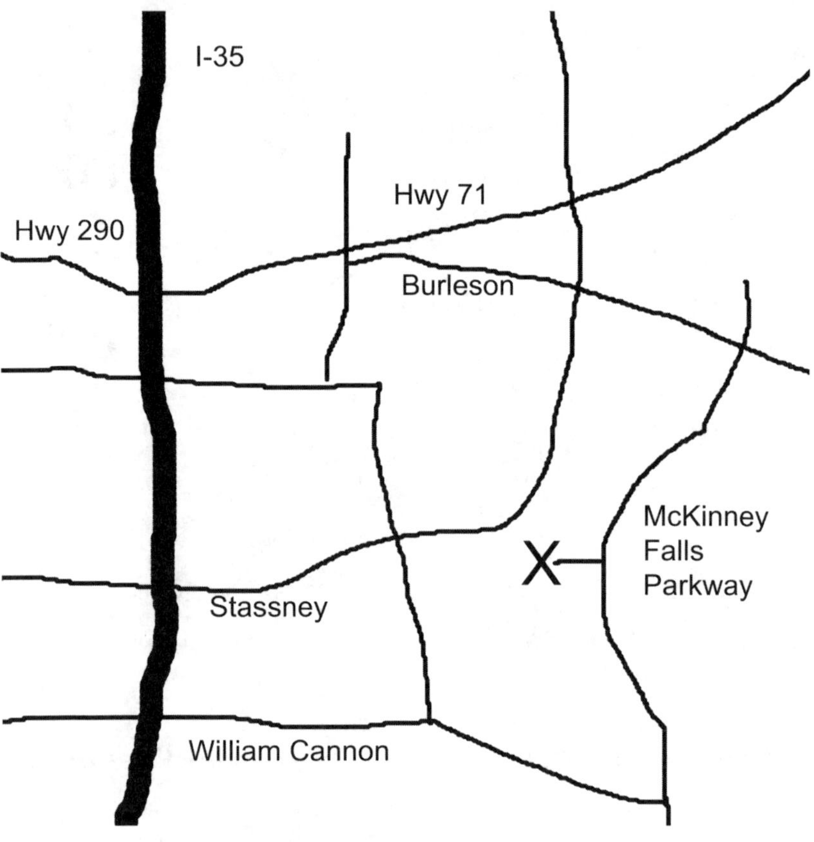

AustinRock
ErockOnline.com

The Roof

The roof is the obvious overhang on the left most side of the rock band. The sand under the roof makes for a nice landing.

1) Wayne's Mantle – (V3)
Start standing on the left end of the roof. A large shelf leads to a slopey highball. Start on a lip 8 ft right of the tree.

2) Backseat Driver   (V5)
Start on the only jugs you will find located in the middle of the roof. Top out straight up.

3) Archimedes Lever (V11)

4) Driving Miss Daisy (V12)

5) Tilted Earth – (V9)
Start sitting near the right end of the roof on a sloper shelf, and move out of the roof into the flake.

6) Unknown
Sit start on a right facing flake and make a big move to a small edge with the left hand and top out.

7) Unknown
Start with a small right facing crimp and dyno for the top.

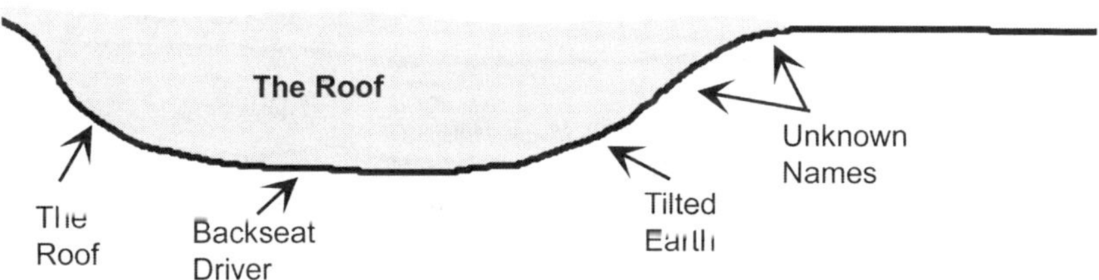

Scrunchy Wall

This is the short wall between the roof and just to the right of
the main access tree. The problems are short, and are mostly all
sit starts.

8) Left Scrunchy Problem – (V?)

Sit start just right of the roof on a flake like cookie edge.
Move up and left.

9) Alterna-Chick – (V4)

Start sitting on a large flat ledge above undercut feet.
Move up through small edges.

10) Low Rider - (V3)

Start sitting on a low small positive edge and hard to find
mono with undercut feet.

11) Dirt Bag – (V2)

Sit start on the lone flat one pad edge.

12) Saturn III – (V6)

This route starts sitting.

13) Naval Power – (V7)

Sit start on dueling slanting jugs. Head up and slightly
right.

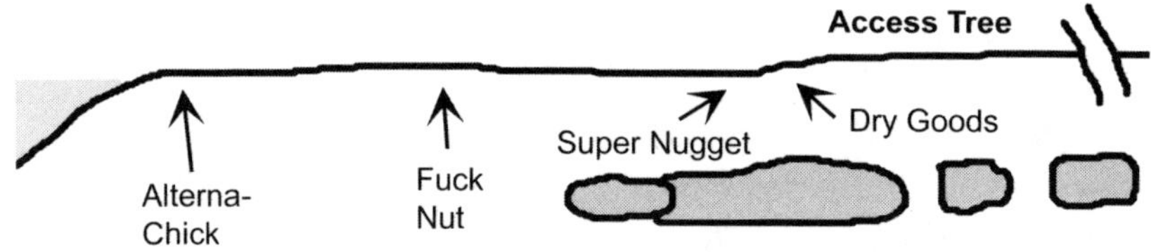

AustinRock
ErockOnline.com

14) Fuck Nut – (V3)

Sit start on a slopey, slanting jug and a small edge.

15) Super Nugget – (V4)

Start sitting on an obvious sloping rail. Move up through side pulls.

16) Dry Goods – (V4)

Start sitting on pockets just left of the tree. Stay left of the large flake.

16) Dryer Goods – (V0)

This route is the same as Dry Goods, but uses the flake.

Injury Wall

The Injury Wall begins to the right of the access tree and ends to the left of the tree at the overhang.

1) Left Most Injury – (V0)

Begin sitting on a slanting edge just right of the thick flake. Move up and slightly left through good pockets.

2) Clingon – (V3)

Start sitting just to the right of "Left Most Injury" on pockets. Move up and slightly left through the finger sprag.

3) Pint Curl – (V3)

Sit start on positive edges. Move up through the under cling mono.

4) Right of Pint Curl – (V4)

Start sitting on jugs and up through pockets

5) Broken Feet – (V4)

Start on a sloper jug/rail and continue up through the large mono.

6) Power Slide Stand – (V5)

Start standing on mono and sloper jug. Move up through a good edge just under the lip.

7) Powerslide – (V7)

This is the direct sit start to the standing variation above.

8) Perineum Blowout Dyno – (V?)

Start standing on shallow monos and lunge for the lip.

9) Perineum Blowout – (V?)

Sit start to above.

10) Power Merchant – (V7)

Start standing on the prominent slot-jug and move up through the textured slope just left of the arête and tree.

11) Power Slut – (V8)

This is a variation to "Power Merchant". Start low on the slopey ledge and good pocket. Finish "Power Merchant".

12) Powerslut Prow Linkup – (V7)

Sit start on "Power Merchant" and finish on the "Prow".

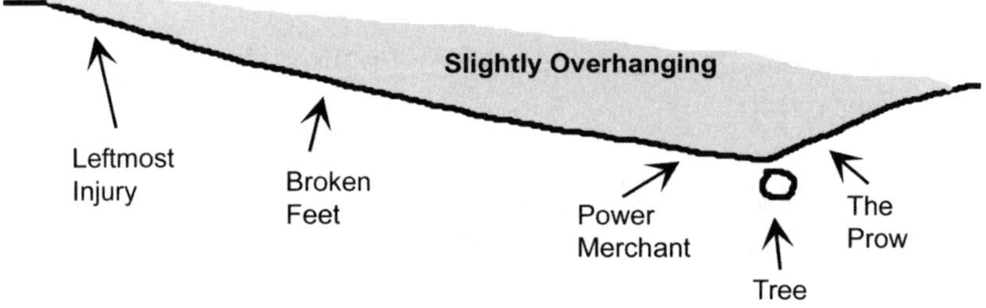

Warm-up Wall

The Warm-up Wall begins to the right of the tree that touches the rock at the top. It is often the most crowded area on busy days, then slowly begins to thin out as the super strong move on to harder areas. The Warm-Up Wall has a large variety of problems spanning the grades.

1) **Prow - Power Merchant Linkup – (V8)**
   Start sitting on "The Prow", move into "Power Merchant" and finish.

2) **Prow – (V4)**
   One of the finest problems around with many variations for the start. Move off the left end of the rail system up left through a jug on right side of the arête. (add a sit down and left on starting feet - V4+)

3) **Unnamed Warm Up Thing – (V2)**
   Start standing from the rail system and move up through a slopey jug and small edges.

4) **Another One Worth Doing – (V2)**
   Start below where the horizontal seem bulges out and gets very juggy, up through a slopey 2 1/2 finger pocket and good two finger pocket. Juggy top out.

5) **Flake Lunge – (V1)**
   Sit just right of "Another One Worth Doing" below the obvious jug flake and go straight up, dynoing for the lip.

6) **Cedar Elm Top Out – (V3)**
   Start standing just left of a small cedar elm and go straight up through a small two finger pocket and over the cedar elm branch to top out.

7) Mono Pop - (V2)

Start standing just right of the tree. Begin on slopey edges and move through the mono side pull.

8) Adam's Jump – (V4)

Start standing and move through shallow pockets and slopey edge.

To the right of "Adam's Jump" is a vertical section of rock with a large undercling flake on the right side. This wall is often used as the warm-up/training wall for McKinney newbie's as it is the only straight vertical section of rock with no overhanging moves.

There are no names for the problems here, but they all fall in the V0 to V2 range.

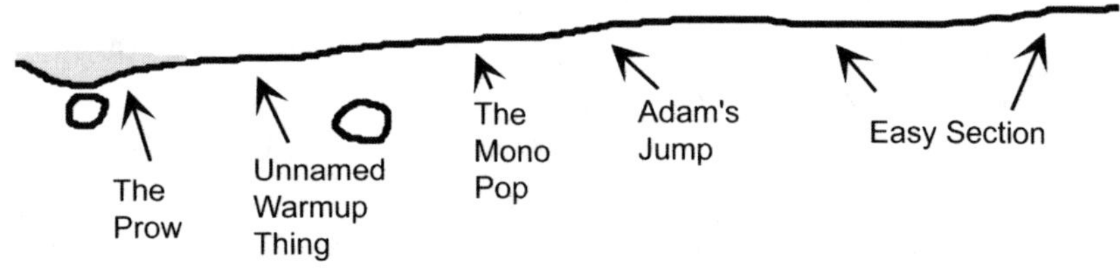

AustinRock

ErockOnline.com

Andy Klier on "Adam's Jump". www.mcrrickales.com

Spacefarm Wall

The Spacefarm Wall starts where the routes become overhanging again to the right of the left facing flake.

1) Local Plates (V4)

Start in a rail system above the poorly located boulder. Move up through dueling sharp pockets.

2) Left El Camino (V6)**

Three feet right of "Local Plates", start in a small pocket system then directly up through small holds to a slopey jug then up and over.

3) Right El Camino (V7)

Start "Evil Eyes" and finish on "Left El Camino".

4) Evil Eyes (V5)***

Perhaps the McKinney classic. Start right of the tree in the pocket band. Move up and right through the obvious two finger sprag under cling.

5) Evil Eyes Direct (V6)

Start directly under the first pocket on "Evil Eyes" and finish "Evil Eyes".

6) Queer Junkies (V8)

Start off a slopey jug in the horizontal seem and mono; Move up and through the crimp and sloper into pockets.

7) Junkie Queers Direct (V8)

Start in the broken ledge below the mono.

8) Siege Tactics (V6)

Start on the two finger pinch left hand and move up and right through slopers.

Dave Teykl on "Left El Camino". www.merrickales.com

9) Blown Clutch (V2)

Sit start to "Double Clutchin" up right dyno to the large dihedral jugs in between "Siege Tactics" and the top out for "Double Clutchin".

10) Double Clutchin' (V4)***

Sit just right of the chossy dihedral and the tree on sharp pockets. Move up through sloping slots and pockets.

11) Trapeze Freak (V8)

Begin on the obvious low side pull and mono; iron cross right through a sloper and up to a lunge.

12) Trapezious Freak (V9)

Add a couple of moves by starting to the left on the large jug and two finger.

13) Jungle Geek (V8)

14) Cirque Du Soleil (V9)

Start under the roof and move up through the sprag, mono and two finger pocket.

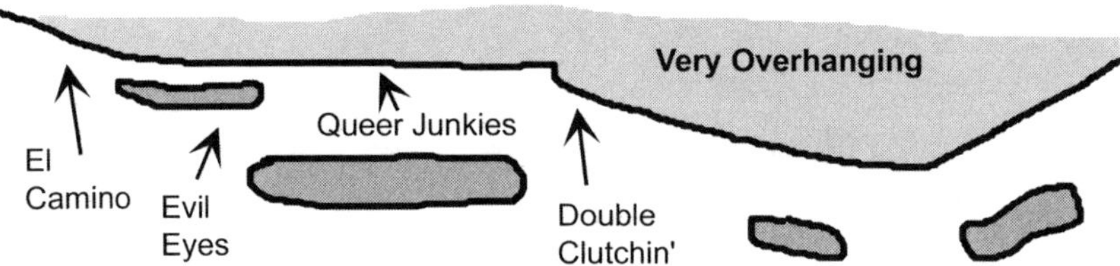

Lunge Wall

The Lunge Wall has a long horizontal crack on the right side of
the large overhang.

1) Lunge Wall Traverse (V3)
Sit at the right most point on the horizontal seem and
traverse left following the seem up and out the dihedral.

2) Uhn ss Uhn ss Uhn ss (V2)
Sit at the right side of the horizontal crack (same as
traverse) up through bad crimps.

3) Stay (V3)
Start on "Uhn ss" start holds and fire up right to a slopey
jug. Difficult variation out right and static to top. Move
bush behind tree for unhindered falls.

Project Wall

The Project wall starts to the right of the huge slanting flake.

1) Fister (V4)
Sit left of the giant sharp flake just right of the stump on
the juggy seem. Go up and over shield.

2) Lubrication For A Fisting (V0)
Sit just right of "Fister" on the same seem up through a big
friendly pocket.

3) Super Fister (V5)
Sit about four feet right of "Lubrication For a Fisting" on
the same juggy seam. Follow the seam up and left and exit
"Fister".

4) Big Sharp Flake (V0)
Traverse up and left on the big sharp flake to a chossy
mantle. Rock is suspect.

5) The Action Is Go (V5)
Start at the base of the flake and move up and right
through funky, small pockets and high edges.

6) Born to Drag (V5)***
Just left of the large cypress tree stand from pocket and
side pull; lunge to the lip.

7) Drag Queen (V6)
Sit start "Born To Drag" on small crimps.

8) Primordial Soup (V6)
This is the pocketed face just left of the arête.

9) Blur (V8)
Start sitting on broken choss up choss covered arête. Most
of this problem has broken off.

10) Sharma Problem - (unrated)
Start on an obvious under cling (blur start) and make
difficult moves past slopers and top out. Poor feet.

11) Kentucky Dream (V4)
Climb up the slopers on the face 6 feet right of the arête
(starting on Blur - V?)

12) Kentucky Cream (V6)
Start on the round, sharp pocket and mono... poor feet

Wet Wall

The Wet Wall is the steep pocketed face to the right of "Kentucky Dream" behind the free standing boulder.

1) Sea Hag (V4)
Move up from the slot and pocket. *Slab wall of left corner is off* (with slab - V0)

2) Kookie Kabuki (V4)

3) Wet Wall Traverse (V7)
Traverse right to left finish on "Sea Hag".

McKinney Proper Boulder

This is the big boulder at the right most part of the wall.

1) Wolf Spider (V2)
Left of the arête in the hallway across from "Kentucky Dream". Contrived sit start in dueling 3 finger pockets about two feet off of the ground up through bad slopers.

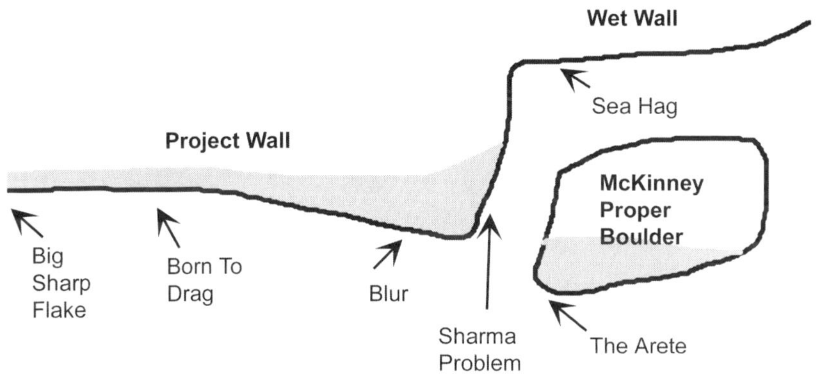

2) The Arête Chicken Exit (V1)

Sit under the arête and exit up and left on the slab.

3) The Arête (V3)

Climb the overhung slopey arête.

4) Whiplash Dyno (V6)

4 feet left of "How Low" sit start on a 2 1/2 finger pocket and slopey crimp out 6 feet to jug on the lip and over.

5) How Low Can You Go (V6)

Begin towards the right side of the overhang beneath the low point of the lip. Start off of good mono under cling.

6) McKinney Boulder Traverse (V?)

Sit on the right side of the boulder. Traverse left across the lip; exit left of the arête.

Melissa Easton on "The Arête". www.merrickales.com

GEORGETOWN HOSPITAL (By Tommy Blackwell)

This hidden gem was developed by Luke Stollings, who worked with the city of Georgetown, the hospital, and the university to gain top rope access to this area. For years that's all there was, and Luke's hard efforts are appreciated as they opened the gateway for future development. In 2002, the Central Texas Mountaineers (CTM) got permission and Southwestern University bought the hardware to bolt many of the top rope lines. Southwestern provides intramural activities for its students including rock climbing. During the Spring and Fall semesters, they will usually be in the area one afternoon a week.

Directions

From Austin, drive north on I-35 and go past Round Rock. Look for the obvious candle factory on the right and take the next exit. This is the exit for the Georgetown hospital. Follow the blue "H" signs to the hospital and park on the right side parking lot of the hospital. Find the small radio antenna behind the main building where you will find a message board and a trail head. Follow the trail down to the shady canyon.

Main Canyon (from right to left)

1) Use the Force Luke (5.11)
Balancing start to the first bolt, after clipping #2 depending on your ape index, either clip #3 or skip it and hit #4. Find the finger pocket in the ceiling, and get ready for the best part. Strong overhanging moves to the 6th bolt. Balance or a dyno is required to clip the chains.

2) Pink Daisy Bunny (5.11 TR)

Set a top rope on "Use the Force Luke". Start by stepping onto a pedestal that is about chest high. Follow the challenging line to the chains.

3) Gateway (5.10)

Start on the rounded arête and clip the first bolt. The 4th bolt is unnecessary if you unlock the top sequence. (4 bolts)

4) The Georgetown Jump (5.10 TR)

With TR set on Gateway, have the climber back up to the trail entrance of the canyon. The belayer stands on the "belay rock" facing AWAY from the climb. The belayer snugs as much stretch out of the rope as possible. Climber and belayer look each other in the eye. When the climber begins running toward the wall, the belayer must run toward the climber and maintain the tight rope. They pass each other at mid point and the belayer turns on the gas. When the climber gets to the edge of the "belay rock" he jumps toward the far away huge ledge. If the belayer has really pulled those final few feet, the climber can "Superman" to the ledge, mantel up and finish the high crux of "Gateway".

5) Blood Sacrifice (5.10+)

Two cruxes make this a fine 5.10

6) Holy Crow (5.11 TR)

Use the top rope anchors, this climb does not top out.

7) Narthex (5.10)

Hard move over the first bolt, non too easy finish. Or use the huge cable TR setup attached to the trees above.

8) Good Book (5.9)

Around the corner to the left is this dihedral. (2 bolts)

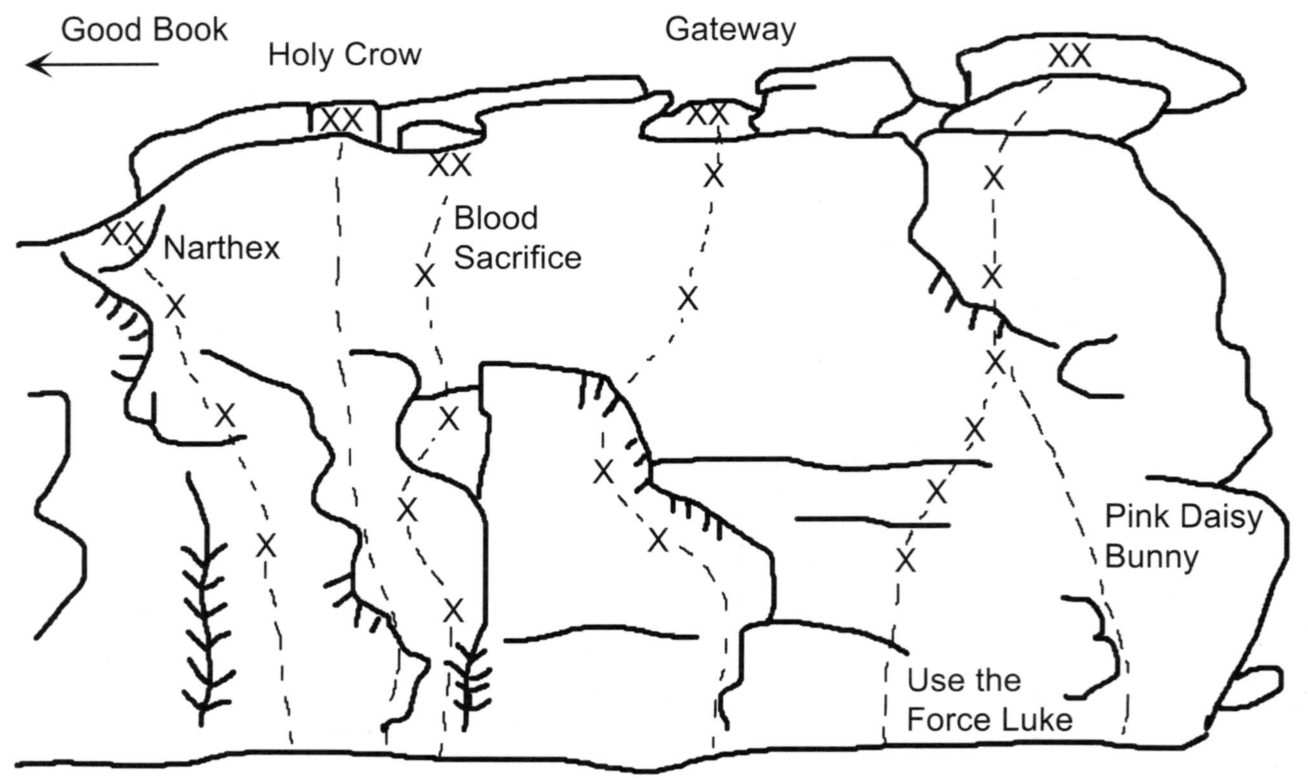

Good Book
Holy Crow
Gateway
Narthex
Blood
Sacrifice
Pink Daisy
Bunny
Use the
Force Luke

The Pulpit

2 bolted lines with multiple variations possible. The bolted lines go about 5.6. There are a total of 10 bolted hangers

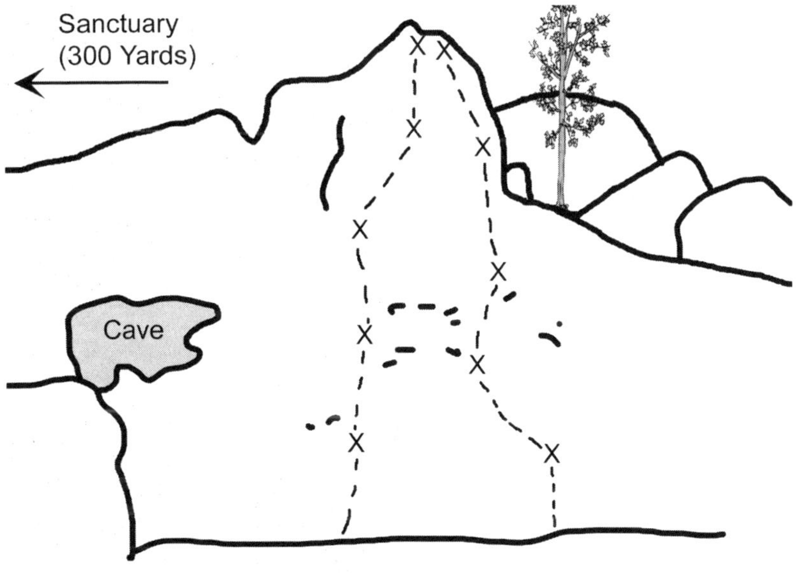

Change Your Altitude
WITH
RockAbout
CLIMBING COURSES AND ADVENTURES
CLIMBING CENTRAL TEXAS LIMESTONE FOR OVER 20 YEARS
AMGA FIELD TESTED
BSA MERIT BADGE CERTIFIED
VISIT OUR WEBSITE FOR PRICING & DESTINATION INFO
1-877-95 CLIMB
www.rock-about.com

TRANGO
available from:
Whole Earth
Provision Co.
Texas
AUSTIN • DALLAS • HOUSTON • SAN ANTONIO
photo: Merrick Ales

AustinRock
ErockOnline.com

Black Diamond™

AustinRock
ErockOnline.com

TL	ROUTE NAME	GRADE	PG
☐	Cedar Elm Topout	(V3)	177
☐ ☐	Cedar Fever	(5.10d)***	69
☐ ☐	Cell Block	(5.11)	51
☐ ☐	Centipede	(5.11a)**	124
☐ ☐	Chain Gang	(5.9)	56
☐ ☐	Champagne and Reefer	(5.12d)	31
☐ ☐	Channel 99	(5.12a)**	67
☐ ☐	Charlie Don't Surf	(5.10d)***	47
☐ ☐	Check Your Head	(5.12c)	155
☐ ☐	Chemical Warfare	(5.11a)	101
☐ ☐	Chicken Supreme	(5.10bTR)	42
☐	Chimney Shorts	(V0-)	91
☐ ☐	Cinching Up the Rootlock	(5.13d)	157
☐	Cirque De Soleil	(V9)	182
☐ ☐	Classic (greenbelt)	(5.4)	78
☐	Classic (bullcreek)	(V0)	92
☐ ☐	Clawing Zoë	(5.7)	128
☐	Clingon	(V3)	175
☐ ☐	Cliptomania	(5.11a)**	131
☐ ☐	Clone Call	(5.9)	152
☐ ☐	Cloud Nine	(5.11d)*	57
☐	Cool Beans Camacho	(V7)	130
☐	Corner Right	(V2)	147
☐ ☐	Crack Ate the Pipe	(5.8)	147
☐ ☐	Crack Attack	(5.10d)	155
☐ ☐	Crack Smack	(5.9)	155
☐ ☐	Crankenstein	(5.11c/d)***	167
	Crankenstein Wall		**163**
☐	Crap Ride	(V5)	96
☐	Creek Side	(V1)	
☐	Crump Traverse	(V4)	93
☐ ☐	Crystal New Persuasion	(5.10c)**	62
☐ ☐	Curious George	(5.12a)	135
☐ ☐	Cyborg	(5.11b)**	38
☐ ☐	Daddy's Girl	(5.10b)	140
☐ ☐	Damasiadas Cervesas	(5.12a)**	152
☐	Dazzling Desperation	(V2)	91
☐ ☐	Dead Cats Don't Meow	(5.10c)**	126
	Dead Cats Annex		**122**
	Dead Cat's Wall		**124**
☐ ☐	Deception Pass	(5.10a)*	138
☐	Dedo Camacho	(V2)	130
☐ ☐	Deep Flow	(5.13a)	53
☐ ☐	Deferred Adjudication	(5.11b)***	131

TL	ROUTE NAME	GRADE	PG
☐ ☐	Deflower Power	(5.12a/b)	156
☐ ☐	Die Hard	(5.10a)**	163
☐	Digitalia	(V6)	129
☐ ☐	Digitron	(5.10c)	129
	Digitron Boulder		**129**
☐ ☐	Dingohead	(5.12b)**	59
☐	Dirt Bag	(V2)	174
☐ ☐	Dirty Rotten Whore	(5.12a)	31
☐ ☐	Discharge	(5.13c)	111
☐ ☐	Disneyland	(5.13)**	63
☐ ☐	Diving for Rocks	(5.10d)***	24
☐ ☐	Do the Right Thing	(5.12a)	101
☐ ☐	Dog on Lag	(5.9)	140
☐ ☐	Donkey Lady	(5.12c)	112
☐ ☐	Don't Hurt the Rock	(5.11)	65
☐ ☐	Dos Vatos	(5.10d)	146
☐	Double Clutchin	(V4)***	182
	Dr. Seuss Wall		**149**
☐	Drag Queen	(V6)	184
☐ ☐	Dragonfly	(5.12d)	156
☐ ☐	Dreamkeeper	(5.13b)	157
☐	Driving Miss Daisy	(V12)	173
☐	Dry Goods	(V4)	175
☐	Dryer Goods	(V0)	175
☐ ☐	Dude From Dallas	(5.8)	87
☐ ☐	Dude, Where's my Hammer	(5.11b)**	165
☐ ☐	Egg Salad Sandwich	(5.10a)	42
☐	Eigen Vector	(V7)	96
☐ ☐	El Presidente	(5.11a)**	137
☐ ☐	El Primero	(5.9)**	122
☐ ☐	Elephant Man	(5.13a)	112
	Enclave		**69**
☐ ☐	Eraser Head	(5.12aTR)*	57
☐ ☐	Evan's Gate	(5.11TR)***	62
☐	Evil Eyes	(V5)***	180
☐	Evil Eyes Direct	(V6)	180
☐ ☐	Evolution of Choss	(5.14a)	157
☐ ☐	Eye of the Storm	(5.11c)	67
☐ ☐	Ezra's Shelf	(5.10d)	140
☐ ☐	Face Off	(5.9)**	34
☐ ☐	Face On	(5.10)**	34
☐	Face the Face	(V2+)	92
	Far Wall		**103**
☐ ☐	Fat Chicks Tryin' to be Sexy	(5.10a)	149
☐ ☐	Fear of Commitment	(5.10)	29
☐ ☐	Fearless	(5.10a)	133
☐ ☐	Femme	(5.13)	51
☐ ☐	Fern Bar	(5.9)***	39
☐ ☐	Ferntasm	(5.10b R)	131

AustinRock
ErockOnline.com

AustinRock
ErockOnline.com

Zack on "Rain Dance". www.merrickales.com

Thank you for buying this guidebook.

Any feedback is appreciated:
erockguide@hotmail.com

FIND THE ERRORS

Here's the challenge:

There are at least 10 big errors in this guidebook. Can you find them? These possible errors will not include any typos, so if you find any, they do not count as an error in this list. If you can find all ten errors (there may be more than 10, but you only have to find 10), email your list to the email address on the previous page. Your name will be listed on ErockOnline.com.

Good Luck!!!

1. __________________________________
2. __________________________________
3. __________________________________
4. __________________________________
5. __________________________________
6. __________________________________
7. __________________________________
8. __________________________________
9. __________________________________
10. __________________________________